TASTE AND SEE

food for the body and soul

TASTE AND SEE

food for the body and soul

A Cookbook
from the Society of
St. Vincent de Paul
Louisiana Edition

TASTE ❧ SEE

food for the body and soul

Published by the Society of St. Vincent de Paul-Baton Rouge

Copyright © 2009 by
The Society of St. Vincent de Paul-Baton Rouge
P.O. Box 127
Baton Rouge, Louisiana 70821
225-383-7837
www.svdpbr.org

Cover image © by Digital Vision/Getty Images
Photography provided by Kleinpeter Photography, Baton Rouge, Louisiana
Design Concept: Rebecca Maher

This cookbook is a collection of favorite recipes, which are not necessarily original recipes.

ISBN: 978-0-9802337-0-4

Edited, Designed, and Produced by

CommunityClassics™

an imprint of

FRP

a wholly owned subsidiary of Southwestern/Great American, Inc.
P.O. Box 305142
Nashville, Tennessee 37230
800-358-0560

Manufactured in the United States of America
First Printing: 2009
10,000 copies

DEDICATION

*The Cookbook Committee dedicates this book
to the people we are blessed to serve.*

"Oh taste and see that the Lord is good: blessed is the man that trusts in Him."
—Psalm 34:8

"We must love our neighbor as being made in the image of God
and as an object of His love."
—Saint Vincent de Paul

"Christianity is not about ideas but about deeds inspired by love."
*—Frederic Ozanam,
founder of the Society of St. Vincent de Paul*

"If you can't feed a hundred people, then feed just one."
—Mother Teresa

"There are people in the world so hungry, that God cannot appear to them
except in the form of bread."
—Mahatma Gandhi

These scripture passages and quotes have inspired and motivated us as we
reviewed, tested, typed, and proofread recipes for this cookbook.
We dedicate this book to the men, women, and children who have been served
or will be served in the future by the Society of St. Vincent de Paul.

*Cookbook Committee
Society of St. Vincent de Paul,
Council of the Diocese of Baton Rouge
Baton Rouge, Louisiana*

Mission Statement

Inspired by Gospel values, the Society of St. Vincent de Paul, a Catholic lay organization, leads women and men to join together to grow spiritually by offering person-to-person service to the needy and suffering in the tradition of its founder, Blessed Frederic Ozanam, and of its patron, St. Vincent de Paul.

As a reflection of the whole family of God, Members, who are known as Vincentians, are drawn from every ethnic and cultural background, age group, and economic level. Vincentians are united in an international society of charity by their spirit of poverty, humility, and sharing, which is nourished by prayer and reflection, mutually supportive gatherings, and adherence to a basic Rule.

Organized locally, Vincentians witness God's love by embracing all works of charity and justice. The Society collaborates with other people of good will in relieving need and addressing its causes, making no distinction in those served, because in them Vincentians see the face of Christ.

CONTENTS

Preface   8

Foreword   9

Recipe Testers & Readers   10

Recipe Contributors   10

History of the Society in Baton Rouge   12

Louisiana's Gumbo   14

Sponsors   16

JOHN FOLSE RECIPES   17

APPETIZERS, SNACKS & BEVERAGES   35

SOUPS, SALADS & BREADS   53

MAIN COURSES   71

VEGETABLES & SIDE DISHES   105

DESSERTS   139

LARGE QUANTITIES   173

APPENDIX   191

    Abbreviations & Equivalents   193

    Helpful Kitchen Hints   194

    Going Green in the Kitchen   197

    Index   199

Order Information   208

Preface

The title of this cookbook, *Taste and See*, was inspired by the psalm and hymn, "Taste and See the Goodness of the Lord." That thought is reflected in our mission statement and in everything we do at St. Vincent de Paul. The Lord's goodness and His presence in the hearts of our supporters enable us to do His work.

We are all members of God's family, and everything we do is part of His plan. When we extend a helping hand, something miraculous takes place. From that moment forward, our lives are connected in ways beyond understanding. We may never meet the people we help, but somehow their lives become a part of ours. These strangers and the hardships they face are experiences we share, and our lives are enriched when we reach out to them. Like a pebble dropped into a pool of water, the effects of our deeds ripple outward from our hands.

Taste and See is much more than a compilation of favorite recipes and stories about the men, women, and children we serve. This publication, we hope, will reach a broad audience of people who share our concern for the poor and homeless and, in turn, generate much-needed resources. Our goal is to educate and enlighten, and in the process, change someone's life—maybe yours.

FOREWORD

"God prospers us not to raise our standard of living, but our standard of giving."

God teaches us that generosity is a way of life, a joyful expression of God's grace. How blessed are we who are able to give from our time and treasure to God's missions, such as St. Vincent de Paul.

It is a privilege for my company and me to support the activities of St. Vincent de Paul through annual projects such as Count Your Blessings and Empty Bowls. We are always thrilled when invited to share a recipe that the talented culinary staff transforms into a hearty meal, and it is an honor when invited to serve the dining room guests. But our participation is only one small part of the generosity that pours from the souls who provide medication for the pharmacy, clothing for the thrift stores, shelter for the homeless, and food for the thousands of meals served from the kitchen. We are humbled by this invitation to serve God's family.

The Society of St. Vincent de Paul has once again honored us by asking for recipes to include in this new cookbook, which is filled with fabulous Louisiana recipes. And more importantly, the proceeds from the cookbook sales will help to finance the many charitable works of the Society.

Once again, my company and I are privileged to "share with God's people who are in need" and to "practice hospitality," as the Lord has directed. Thank you, St. Vincent de Paul, for the blessing that you are to us.

"Give, and it will be given to you. A good measure, pressed down, shaken together and running over, will be poured into your lap. For with the measure you use, it will be measured to you." Luke 6:38

Chef John D. Folse
Owner/Executive Chef
Chef John Folse & Company

Recipe Testers & Readers

Ivy & Kitty Alford
Amy Arnold
Edith Babin
George & Kathy Bishop
Esma Brougham
Marion Brown
Vickie Calloway
Bob & Judy Cancienne
Cheryl Cochran
Helen Cole
Jerry & Blanche Daigre
Pat Davenport
Barbara Delaville
Lucille Dunn
Debra Eidson
Nikki Eidson

Nancy Endom
Tami Flynn
Israel Garcia
Jerrie Guillory
Bill & Barbara Holden
Mary Karam
Lisa Knotts
Dyer & Joyce LaFleur
Judy LeJeune
Ginger Lowery
Carolyn McCalip
Gloria McDaniel
Phyllis McKay
Gary & Rosemary Meier
Eve Mitchell
Jenny Morales

Mary Morgan
Dianne Muchow
Joyce Nicolle
Leola Ourso
Barbara Pecora
Janice Penton
Joan Pinell
Connie Planche
Jane Quinn
Cindy Ristroph
Mary Kay Schuessler
Betty Simino
Denise Spears
Crystal Stelly
Diane Tonkovich
Bob & Jan Wilson

Recipe Contributors

Ivy Alford
Kitty Alford
Yvonne Andrews
Mary Ann Antrobus
Edith Babin
Jane Bahlinger
Josie Barcelona
Kerry Bardell
Father Jeff Bayhi
Margaret Bayhi
Modie Bennett
Ainsley Bishop

Kathy Bishop
Marina Bishop
Jim & Smittie Bolner
Mr. & Mrs. Jim
    Bolton, Sr.
Lisa Brannan
Frances Breaux
Helen Brown
Marion Brown
Will Browning
Sr. Josephine Caballero
Juanita Cacippo

Vickie Calloway
Janice Caston
Crystal Chatelain
Lamy Chopin
Shirley Chustz
Holly Clegg
Kirt Clement
Commander's Palace
Judy Concienne
Juanita Coutee
Blanche Daigre
Pat Davenport

Jan deGravelles
Barbara Delaville
Bonnie DeSilva
Shirley Doyle
Fran Edwards
Debra Eidson
Gladys Eidson
Nikki Eidson
Carla Fair
Tami Flynn
Chef John Folse
Jodi & Keith Fryoux
Tiffany Garland
Melinda Germany
Jean Glyson
Joycelyn Green
Sandy Guidry
Jerrie Guillory
Mary Hall
Hands On Baton Rouge
Elaine Harelson
Ron Hebert
Barbara Holden
Maria Horcasitas
Trudy Huffty
Sonia Hunt
Joan Jardell
Cindy Junot
Dot Keesing
John Kirkwood
Leon Kleinpeter, Jr.
Lisa Knotts
Joyce Lafleur

Lena Lanclos
Dorothy Langreck
Myrtis Leonard
Louisiana Lagniappe
LSU Human Ecology
    Department
CoCo Martin
Page Meyer
Jason Mike
Lisa Miller
Eve Mitchell
Becky Mixon
Mary Morgan
Kathy Morris
Dianne Muchow
Candy Muse
Barbara Pecora
Janice Penton
Eloise Persac
Earline Pesdon
Connie Planche
Terri Porter
Pat Prince
Louis & Jane Quinn
Pamela Rhodes
Christine Richardson
Robert J. Rolfsen, Sr.
Beth Scardina
Zoe Schluter
Mary Kay Schuessler
Jeanette Silvio
Margaret Simino
Gertie Smith

Myra Smith
Lucy Sullivan
Irene Thibodeaux
Gary Tullier
Fulton Toaston
Tony's Seafood
Lisa Town
Louise Tricon
Mardie Varner
Penny Vicknair
Perry Williams
Kathleen Willoughby
Jan Wilson
Fr. George Wiltz

11

HISTORY OF THE SOCIETY
IN BATON ROUGE

The Society of St. Vincent de Paul is an international nonprofit organization founded in 1833 by Blessed Frederic Ozanam in Paris, France.

Since 1865, St. Vincent de Paul has had a rich history of service to the needy in the Baton Rouge area. Our mission, through person-to-person contact, mass feeding, sheltering, and other channels, encompasses every form of aid that alleviates suffering and promotes dignity and integrity. All races, creeds, colors, origins, castes, opinions, and genders are served.

Presently, we support a variety of programs that provide critically needed services, including food, clothing, shelter, and healthcare, to the poorest of the poor. Our St. Vincent de Paul Conference members, called Vincentians, make home visits to those requesting assistance with these basic needs.

Throughout the years our ability to provide these critical services has been due to the overwhelming support of the community. The many milestones include the following:

In 1963, the Society in Baton Rouge started a thrift store program. Today, we operate eight thrift stores throughout the community, offering a broad range of gently used household items at minimal cost to the patrons. The revenues generated support our various charitable outreach programs. The stores provide clothing, furniture, and household items free of charge to those who qualify, touching thousands of lives every year.

In 1982, our Society recognized the growing number of the homeless and poor who were suffering from hunger and opened the St. Vincent de Paul Dining Room. The dining room now serves more than 200,000 meals annually, providing a hot nutritious meal to those who would otherwise go without *any* meal.

In 1991, the Society established the Bishop Ott Shelter housing program to provide shelter for homeless men. Today, our programs for the homeless include a day center, two emergency shelters for men, the Sweet Dreams Shelter for women and children, and Myriam's House, which provides transitional housing for women. Annually, our shelters provide more than 20,000 guest nights of shelter in a safe and comfortable environment.

In 1995, the Society responded to the need for assistance with prescription medicine by opening the St. Vincent de Paul Community Pharmacy. The pharmacy fills more than 30,000 prescriptions annually with an estimated value of approximately $2 million a year. This program is a safety net for those who cannot afford their life-sustaining prescription medications.

Throughout the years our Society has responded to the needs of the most vulnerable in our community, and we are committed to continue serving in this ever-changing environment.

LOUISIANA'S GUMBO

Chef John Folse has stated that this book is filled with "fabulous Louisiana recipes." But what makes Louisiana recipes unique?

We would like to think that if the United States is a melting pot of cultures, then Louisiana is the ladle that creates, stirs up, and serves a wonderful blend of spices, methods, and traditions of cooking.

Creole cooking had its roots in New Orleans as early as 1751. The French word *creoles*, or Spanish *criollo*, literally translates to "native to the place." The earliest settlers from France and Spain brought their recipes and methods of cooking with them, but the spices and other ingredients they used were often "native to the place." Then local Native American tribes taught the early settlers how to prepare much of the seafood and game found in Louisiana and how to cook with indigenous roots, herbs, and spices, such as the filé (dried sassafras leaves) used to thicken gumbo.

In 1755, the "Cajuns" were exiled by the British from Acadia, a French colony in eastern Canada. Many of these "Acadians," or Cajuns, settled near St. Martinville in South Louisiana. Unlike the settlers in New Orleans, a port city, the Cajuns could not rely on imported goods and had to learn to cook what the land, the swamps, and the bayous provided.

Soon, other cultures, attracted by the rich farmland, settled the area along the Mississippi River between New Orleans and Baton Rouge. By the late eighteenth century, German immigrants were farming near what is now des Allemands (French for "the Germans") and incorporating their know-how for sausage making into the local cuisine. When Italian immigrants settled in various cities throughout the state, they too brought with them their recipes and celebrations. Irish settlers first put down their roots in the early 1800s in New Orleans, and to this day, they celebrate St. Patrick's Day not with just a parade but with "throws" of cabbage and potatoes to go into the Irish stew.

While a community known as "Hungarian Settlement" was growing up east of Baton Rouge, Scots and English were developing the land to the north of Baton Rouge. Puddings and pies reflect what this land produced in the way of fresh fruits, vegetables, and rich dairy products.

Settlers in North Louisiana came to the area primarily from other eastern and southern states, in 1803, when Louisiana was sold to the United States. They brought with them the techniques of cooking and the recipes that more closely resemble the traditional style of southern cooking, such as corn breads, chicken and dumplings, and biscuits and white gravy.

Enriching this growing mix of cultures and tastes in food, Africans introduced their own flavors, knowledge of spices, and foods unknown to the European settlers, but readily available in Louisiana. Yam dishes are but one example of this culinary gift!

Some immigrants to Louisiana came as large groups, such as those from Haiti in the early 1800s, and later Cubans and Vietnamese in the middle to late 1900s. Other peoples, such as the Lebanese, Greeks, East Indians, and those from Central and South America, came as family groups, always bringing with them their special recipes and ways of cooking to blend in a special way with the rich heritage of Louisiana cuisine.

Over the years, Baton Rouge cooks have drawn on all these recipes and methods of cooking. Some of the recipes in *Taste and See* have been simplified by using more convenient ingredients and techniques, but the essential tastes have been preserved.

Finally, as far as most Louisianans are concerned, a life without their faith would be like a gumbo without salt. Generations of Catholics, Jews, and Protestants have celebrated religious holidays and fellowship with feasts of sumptuous foods. From special Passover meals, to Baptist church homecomings with "dinner on the ground," to Papa Noel Feasts shared around a bonfire, gatherings in Louisiana always seem to include food, and what better way to taste and see the goodness of the Lord?

EXECUTIVE CHEF SPONSORS

Anonymous
George & Kathy Bishop
Mr. & Mrs. Donald Broussard
Fred & Shannon Cerise
Michael & Kathleen Crapanzano
In Honor of Dorothy & Walter Morales and Jean & James O'Beirne
Pelican State Credit Union
In Memory of David & Lorraine Planche
Pat Ruckstuhl
Roy & Ruby Schnebelen
Tony's Seafood Market & Deli and Louisiana Fish Fry Products
Bert & Sue Turner
In Memory of Guy Waggenspack
Michael & Marie Walsh
4th Sunday Shelter Supper Group

CHEF SPONSORS

Paul Burton
Sam & Phyllis Cancienne
Coca-Cola of Baton Rouge
Cathy & David Doran
Friends of St. Vincent de Paul
Dr. J. D. Guillory
Hannis T. Bourgeois, CPAs
Francis & Robin Jumonville
Robert & Cheryl Kirchoff
Doug & Susan Nelson
Kathy & Stephen Shirley
Eulis & Tammy Simien
Sissy & Ralph Stevens

John Folse
Recipes

COUNT YOUR BLESSINGS

Food is so much more than sustenance for the body. It nourishes and nurtures, comforts and consoles. There are few things more rewarding than preparing a favorite meal for your family; welcoming a new neighbor with a homemade pound cake; trying a new recipe as an excuse to have friends over; and making soup for a sick friend to convey love and care. These actions of a caring heart go far beyond meeting nutritional needs.

At our annual Count Your Blessings Supper, the simple meal and evening shared are filled with symbolism. This fund-raising event is held during Lent, a time of self-reflection and inner growth, in response to the great sacrifice made more than two thousand years ago. The supper serves as a reminder of our blessings and our responsibility to help those in the community who suffer from hunger.

At St. Vincent de Paul, one of the many blessings for which we are thankful is our friend and longtime supporter Chef John Folse. The Count Your Blessings Supper would not be possible without his willingness to share his time, talent, and treasure with our organization and the larger community in which he lives and works. He exemplifies the love, compassion, and commitment that are at the heart of the Vincentian way of life.

We are extremely grateful to Chef Folse and to every volunteer and supporter who shares our common concern for the poor and homeless. While we count our blessings for all that has been given to our organization, we are most thankful for the opportunity to serve God's poor, for in them we see the face of Christ.

Pan-Seared Trout with Crab Meat Garlic Beurre Blanc

1 pound jumbo lump crab meat
1 egg
1/2 cup milk
1/2 cup water
2 cups all-purpose flour
Salt and black pepper to taste
Granulated garlic to taste
1/2 cup vegetable oil
6 (6-ounce) speckled trout fillets
1/4 cup julienned andouille

1/4 cup sliced green onions
1/4 cup sliced mushrooms
2 tablespoons minced garlic
1/4 cup (1/2 stick) butter, melted
1/4 cup dry white wine
1/2 cup heavy whipping cream
3/4 cup (1 1/2 sticks) cold
  butter, chopped
White pepper to taste

Pick through the crab meat gently, discarding any bits of shell or cartilage; set aside. Mix the egg, milk and water in a shallow dish. Place the flour in a shallow dish. Season with salt, black pepper and granulated garlic. Heat the oil in large heavy skillet over medium-high heat. Dip the trout in the egg mixture and then immediately dredge in the flour mixture. Cook in the hot oil for 6 to 10 minutes or until golden brown and the fish begins to flake, turning once. Remove from the heat and keep warm.

Sauté the sausage, green onions, mushrooms and garlic in 1/4 cup butter for 3 to 5 minutes or until tender. Add the wine and cook until reduced by half, stirring constantly and scraping up any brown bits from the bottom of the skillet. Add the cream and cook until reduced by half. Fold in the crab meat, reserving a small amount for garnish. Add 3/4 cup butter gradually, stirring constantly with a wooden spoon until combined. Remove from the heat and season with salt and white pepper. Spoon generous portions of the sauce in the center of six 10-inch dinner plates. Arrange the trout over the sauce and garnish with the reserved crab meat.

Serves 6

Compound butter sauces are part of the way of life in south Louisiana. Though similar in method, each sauce has its own ingredients that make it unique. This classic beurre blanc is flavored Louisiana-style with lump crab meat and andouille.

Crab Cakes Rex

1 pound lump crab meat
$1/2$ cup chopped onion
$1/2$ cup chopped celery
$1/2$ cup chopped red bell pepper
$1/4$ cup minced garlic
3 tablespoons butter
1 cup Italian bread crumbs
$1/4$ cup thinly sliced green onions
$1/4$ cup mayonnaise
1 egg, lightly beaten

2 tablespoons minced parsley
2 teaspoons lemon juice
2 teaspoons Worcestershire sauce
2 tablespoons Old Bay seasoning
1 teaspoon Creole mustard
Tabasco sauce to taste
Granulated garlic to taste
Salt and cracked pepper to taste
$1/2$ cup Italian bread crumbs
$1/4$ cup vegetable oil

Pick through the crab meat gently, discarding any bits of shell or cartilage; set aside. Sauté the onion, celery, bell pepper and minced garlic in the butter in a skillet for 3 to 5 minutes or until tender. Remove to a mixing bowl and let stand until slightly cool. Stir in 1 cup Italian bread crumbs, the green onions, mayonnaise, egg, parsley, lemon juice, Worcestershire sauce, Old Bay seasoning and Creole mustard. Season with hot sauce, granulated garlic, salt and black pepper. Fold in the crab meat by hand. Adjust the seasonings to taste. Shape the crab mixture into patties 1 inch thick and $2^1/2$ inches wide. Dust with $1/2$ cup bread crumbs and arrange on a dish. Chill, covered, for 1 hour. Heat the oil in a skillet over medium heat. Add the crab cakes and cook for 4 to 6 minutes or until golden brown and heated through, turning once. Serve with white remoulade sauce or red remoulade sauce.

Serves 8

The crab cakes of Bayou country are usually dense in texture due to the abundance of bread crumbs in the recipes. For a more appetizing texture, this recipe has fewer bread crumbs and more crab meat.

Barbecued Shrimp Longman

48 (21-to 25-count) shrimp, heads on
1 tablespoon light margarine
1 tablespoon olive oil
4 garlic cloves, minced
1/3 cup Worcestershire sauce
Hot red pepper sauce to taste
1 teaspoon paprika
Granulated garlic to taste
Salt and pepper to taste
1/4 cup chopped parsley

Arrange the shrimp in a single layer on a rimmed baking pan; set aside. Combine the margarine, olive oil, garlic, Worcestershire sauce, hot sauce, paprika, granulated garlic, salt and pepper in a saucepan. Cook for 1 to 2 minutes, stirring constantly. Add the parsley and cook for 1 minute longer, stirring constantly. Pour over the shrimp. Bake at 350 degrees for 10 to 15 minutes, turning the shrimp occasionally. Pour into a large ceramic serving bowl. Serve with toasted French bread.

Serves 6

Barbecued shrimp originated at Manale's Restaurant in New Orleans. Customers waiting for the next tables formed long lines down Napoleon Avenue. Perfecting the flavor of barbecued shrimp can be difficult for culinary novices and masters alike, but eating this tasty dish is sure to be an enjoyable, although messy, experience.

Louisiana Clam Chowder

1 cup minced onion
1 cup minced celery
1/4 cup minced red bell pepper
1 tablespoon minced garlic
1/2 cup (1 stick) butter
6 tablespoons all-purpose flour
5 cups clam juice
2 cups milk

1 1/2 cups heavy cream
1 teaspoon chopped fresh thyme
2 cups chopped potatoes
1/4 cup chopped fresh parsley
Salt and pepper to taste
1 (16-ounce) can clams, drained
    and chopped

Sauté the onion, celery, bell pepper and garlic in the butter in a 2-quart saucepan for 3 to 5 minutes or until tender. Whisk in the flour. Whisk in the clam juice, milk and cream. Add the thyme and bring to a gentle boil. Reduce the heat and simmer for 15 minutes, stirring occasionally. Add the potatoes, parsley, salt and pepper. Simmer until the potatoes are tender. Add the clams and simmer until the clams are heated through. Serve with crackers or French bread.

Serves 6 to 8

Chef John Folse and Company prepares a Lenten meal of soup and bread for the annual Count Your Blessings supper. It has been an honor and a privilege to work with Chef Folse for the past thirteen years on this important event.

Louisiana-Style Crawfish Étouffée

1/2 cup (1 stick) butter
1 cup chopped onion
1/2 cup chopped celery
1/2 cup chopped green bell pepper
1/2 cup chopped red bell pepper
1/2 cup chopped tomatoes
2 tablespoons minced garlic
2 bay leaves
1 cup all-purpose flour
1/2 cup tomato sauce

2 pounds shelled crawfish tails
2 quarts crawfish stock or water
2 tablespoons sherry
1 cup sliced green onions
1/2 cup chopped parsley
Salt and cayenne pepper to taste
2 cups hot steamed white rice
2 to 3 dashes hot red pepper sauce, or
  to taste

Melt the butter in a 2-gallon stockpot over medium-high heat. Add the onion, celery, green bell pepper, red bell pepper, tomatoes, garlic and bay leaves. Sauté for 3 to 5 minutes or until the vegetables are tender. Add the flour and whisk until combined and the flour is no loner grainy. Stir in the tomato sauce and crawfish tails. Cook for 5 minutes, stirring constantly. Add the stock gradually, stirring constantly until of a sauce consistency. Bring to a boil. Reduce the heat and simmer for 30 minutes, stirring occasionally and adding additional stock as needed to retain the sauce consistency. Stir in the sherry, green onions and parsley. Simmer for 5 minutes. Remove and discard the bay leaves. Season with salt and cayenne pepper. Serve over the rice. Season with hot sauce.

Serves 6

The French word, étouffée means to stew, smother, or braise. This technique is found in dishes using shrimp, crab, crawfish, meat, or game. Though more Creole in origin, étouffées are found throughout Louisiana.

Louisiana Seafood Gumbo

12 cups shellfish stock
1 cup vegetable oil
1 cup all-purpose flour
2 cups chopped onions
1 cup chopped celery
1 cup chopped bell pepper
$1/4$ cup minced garlic
8 ounces andouille, sliced
1 pound (35-count) shrimp, peeled
   and deveined

1 pound claw crab meat
1 cup chopped frozen okra
2 cups sliced green onions
$1/2$ cup chopped parsley
Salt and cayenne pepper to taste
Tabasco sauce to taste
1 pound jumbo lump crab meat
2 dozen shucked oysters,
   liquid reserved
Hot cooked rice

Heat the stock in a saucepan. Heat the oil in a 7-quart saucepan or stockpot over medium heat. Whisk in the flour and cook until light brown, whisking constantly. Add the onions, celery, bell pepper and garlic. Sauté for 3 to 5 minutes or until the vegetables are tender. Add the sausage and sauté for 3 to 5 minutes. Stir in $1/2$ cup of the shrimp, the claw crab meat and okra. Add the hot stock gradually, stirring constantly until the desired consistency is reached. Bring to a gentle boil and reduce the heat. Simmer for 30 minutes. Add additional stock as needed to maintain the consistency. Stir in the green onions and parsley. Season with salt, cayenne pepper and hot sauce. Fold in the remaining shrimp, lump crab meat and oysters with liquid. Bring to a gentle boil and cook for 5 minutes longer. Adjust the seasoning to taste. Serve over hot cooked rice.

Serves 12

Seafood Gumbo is the premier soup of Cajun country and it is known worldwide as the dish to seek out when visiting south Louisiana. Every Louisiana home has its own unique ingredients and method for preparing gumbo.

Smoked Wood Duck and Andouille Gumbo

3 wood ducks
1 pound andouille, sliced
16 cups water
1 cup vegetable oil
1 1/4 cups all-purpose flour
2 cups chopped onions
2 cups chopped celery
1/2 cup chopped green bell pepper
1/2 cup chopped red bell pepper
1/2 cup chopped yellow bell pepper

1/4 cup minced garlic
Hot red pepper sauce to taste
Creole seasoning to taste
Granulated garlic to taste
Salt and pepper to taste
2 cups sliced green onions
1 cup chopped parsley
2 tablespoons filé powder
Hot steamed white rice

Smoke the ducks until rare in a home-style smoker according to the manufacturer's directions. Cut the ducks into halves. Combine the ducks, sausage and water in a 2-gallon stockpot. Bring to a rolling boil over medium-high heat. Boil for 30 to 45 minutes. Drain, reserving the liquid. Let the ducks cool enough to handle. Chop the ducks, discarding the skin and bones. Combine the ducks and sausage; set aside. Heat the oil in a large heavy saucepan over medium-high heat. Add the flour and cook until dark brown, whisking constantly. Add the onions, celery, green bell pepper, red bell pepper, yellow bell pepper and garlic. Cook until the vegetables are tender, stirring constantly. Stir in the duck and sausage. Add 12 cups of the reserved cooking liquid one ladle at a time until a soup consistency is reached, stirring well after each addition. Bring to a rolling boil. Reduce the heat and simmer for 45 minutes, seasoning with the hot sauce, Creole seasoning, granulated garlic, salt and pepper twice during cooking. Stir in the green onions, parsley and filé powder. Simmer for 5 minutes longer. Serve over hot steamed white rice.

Serves 6

Almost every species of wild game in Louisiana has been used to make gumbo. Most Cajun men were hunters and trappers, so it is not surprising that wild duck and andouille were often used. Often hunters visiting Reid-Toerner House in Lake Charles, Louisiana, contribute wood ducks from the morning hunt and pair it with smoked andouille to create a magnificent gumbo for the evening meal.

Claire's Baked Duck Liver Pâté

8 slices bacon
2 pounds duck livers or chicken livers, drained
Granulated garlic to taste
Salt and pepper to taste
6 garlic cloves, sliced
2 bay leaves
8 ounces cream cheese, softened
^{1}/2 cup (1 stick) unsalted butter, softened
^{1}/4 cup Cognac or white wine

Line a baking dish with the bacon. Add the duck livers and season with granulated garlic, salt and pepper. Tuck the garlic cloves and bay leaves into the center of the duck livers. Bake, covered, at 375 degrees for 45 to 60 minutes or until the center reaches 165 degrees. Let stand for 1 hour or until slightly warm. Remove and discard the bay leaves.

Remove the bacon, duck livers, garlic and pan juices to a food processor. Add the cream cheese, butter and Cognac. Process until smooth and creamy. Season with salt and pepper. Spoon into a decorative serving bowl. Chill, covered, for 4 to 6 hours. Serve with crackers or French bread croutons.

Serves 12 to 15

This recipe is borrowed from my favorite cousin. This rich, flavorful, and inexpensive spread is simple to make and perfect for holiday or family gatherings. It can be prepared a day ahead, but for the best flavor it should be consumed within 2 to 3 days. As with all liver-based dishes, the flavor becomes more pronounced after time.

Mama's Chicken Fricassee

1 (3-pound) chicken, cut up
Tabasco sauce to taste
Salt and pepper to taste
1 cup all-purpose flour
1 cup (or more) vegetable oil
1/2 cup all-purpose flour
2 cups chopped onions
1 cup chopped celery

1/2 cup chopped bell pepper
1 tablespoon minced garlic
6 cups (or more) chicken stock
1 cup sliced mushrooms
1 cup sliced green onions
1/4 cup chopped parsley
1 cup sour cream
Hot steamed rice or hot cooked pasta

Season the chicken with hot sauce, salt and pepper. Dredge the chicken in 1 cup flour, shaking off any excess. Heat 1 cup oil in a large deep skillet over medium-high heat. Fry the chicken in the hot oil in batches until golden brown, turning occasionally. Adjust the heat as needed. Remove the chicken to a dish, reserving the drippings in the skillet. Add additional oil to the pan if needed to make 1/2 cup drippings. Add 1/2 cup flour and cook until golden brown, whisking constantly. Add the onions, celery, bell pepper and garlic. Cook for 3 to 5 minutes or until the vegetables are tender, stirring frequently. Add the stock gradually, whisking constantly. Add the fried chicken and mushrooms and bring to a rolling boil. Reduce the heat and simmer for 45 minutes or until the chicken is cooked through and tender. Add additional stock as needed to reach the desired consistency. Stir in the green onions, parsley and sour cream. Season with hot sauce, salt and pepper. Serve over hot steamed rice.

Serves 6

The best fricassee is made like Mama's, in an old cast-iron pot. Mama would always fry her chicken first, and many times she had to fry extra because the kids would eat it before it got to the stew. In Louisiana, it is traditional to finish fricassee with sour cream.

Medallions of Venison with Kumquat Glaze

13 (3-ounce) medallions of venison
   tenderloin or venison backstrap
Granulated garlic to taste
Salt and pepper to taste
1/4 cup vegetable oil
1/4 cup minced shallots

1/4 cup minced jalapeño chiles
1/2 cup dry red wine
1/2 cup kumquat preserves or
   orange marmalade
1 cup venison or veal Demi-Glace
   (see below)

Season the venison with granulated garlic, salt and pepper. Heat the oil in a 10-inch skillet over medium-high heat. Cook the venison in batches of four in the oil until medium-rare and golden brown on all sides. Remove to a dish, reserving the drippings in the pan; keep warm. Add the shallots and jalapeño chiles to the reserved drippings. Sauté for 1 to 2 minutes or until tender. Add the wine, stirring constantly and scraping up any brown bits from the bottom of the skillet. Stir in the preserves and Demi-Glace. Bring to a boil and reduce the heat to a simmer. Add the venison and simmer until heated through, turning occasionally. Place two medallions on each dinner plate. Spoon the sauce over the top.

Serves 6

Demi-Glace

8 cups beef stock, venison stock or
   veal stock
1/2 cup White Roux (see page 29)

2 tablespoons tomato sauce
2 tablespoons sherry or brandy
   (optional)

Divide the stock between two heavy saucepans and bring both to a gentle boil. Add the White Roux to one saucepan and cook until thickened, whisking constantly. Whisk in the tomato sauce. Simmer, adding hot stock from the second saucepan as the sauce reduces, replacing the volume until all of the stock is used and the volume is reduced to about 4 cups. Strain through a cheesecloth or fine sieve. Stir in the sherry.

Makes 1 quart

Butter Roux

1 cup (2 sticks) butter
1 cup all-purpose flour

To prepare a White Roux, melt the butter over medium-high heat in a heavy saucepan. Add the flour and cook until combined and bubbly, whisking constantly. Do not brown. Use this roux for béchamel sauces, cream sauces and soups.

To prepare a Blond Roux, melt the butter over medium-high heat in a heavy saucepan. Add the flour and cook until pale gold, whisking constantly. Use this roux to thicken étouffées or vegetables dishes, such as butter beans or petits pois.

To prepare a Brown Roux, melt the butter over medium-high heat in a heavy saucepan. Add the flour and cook until light brown, whisking constantly. Discard the sauce and start again if brown flecks appear in the roux. Use this roux to thicken gravies and sauces.

Add the following proportions of stock gradually to the roux to thicken to the desired consistency, stirring constantly. Add 6 cups stock for a white sauce consistency. Add 8 cups stock for a concentrated soup consistency. Add 10 cups stock for a soup consistency. Add 12 cups stock for a perfect Louisiana gumbo consistency. Add 14 cups stock for a light gumbo consistency.

Makes about 2 cups

Butter roux was made in New Orleans by the Creoles. They had access to volumes of butter from vendors in the marketplace. Cajuns traditionally used butter on hot French bread. They considered it wasteful to use good butter in a roux.

Traditional Venison Jerky

2 pounds lean venison
1/2 cup liquid smoke
1/2 cup Worcestershire sauce
1/4 cup teriyaki sauce
1/4 cup soy sauce
1/4 cup hot red pepper sauce
2 tablespoons brown sugar
2 tablespoons cane syrup
2 tablespoons Creole seasoning
2 tablespoons granulated garlic
1 1/2 teaspoons meat tenderizer
1 1/2 teaspoons salt

Slice the venison thinly against the grain. Whisk the liquid smoke, Worcestershire sauce, teriyaki sauce, soy sauce, hot sauce, brown sugar, cane syrup, Creole seasoning, garlic, meat tenderizer and salt in a bowl. Add the venison and toss to coat. Chill, covered, for 24 hours. Place in a dehydrator and cook according to the manufacturer's directions. This process should take approximately 9 hours.

Makes 1 pound

Smoking or dry-curing game meat was a way of preserving the ample harvest. As certain dishes made their way from the hunting camps to the home, variations of flavors were created by different cultures. In this recipe, Asian influence is seen in the addition of teriyaki sauce and soy sauce.

Bayouland Beef Stew with Vegetables

3 pounds beef chuck, cut into cubes
Hot red pepper sauce to taste
Salt and pepper to taste
1/3 cup all-purpose flour
1/4 cup vegetable oil
1 cup chopped onion
1 cup chopped celery
1/2 cup celery leaves
1/4 cup minced garlic

1 bay leaf
2 tablespoons Worcestershire sauce
4 cups hot water or hot beef stock
1 pound carrots, sliced
2 pounds new potatoes, quartered
1 pound mushrooms, sliced
1 cup sliced green onions
1/2 cup chopped parsley
Hot steamed white rice

Place the beef in a large bowl. Season with hot sauce, salt and pepper. Add the flour and toss to coat. Heat the oil in a large heavy saucepan over medium-high heat. Add the beef and cook until brown on all sides, stirring occasionally. Remove with a slotted spoon to a dish and keep warm, reserving the drippings in the pan. Add the onions, celery, celery leaves and garlic to the reserved drippings. Sauté for 3 to 5 minutes or until tender. Add the beef, bay leaf and Worcestershire sauce. Add the water and bring to a boil, stirring constantly and scraping up any brown bits from the bottom of the saucepan. Reduce the heat and simmer, covered, for 1 hour or until the meat is almost tender. Stir in the carrots and potatoes. Simmer for 30 minutes. Stir in the mushrooms, green onions and parsley. Adjust seasonings. Simmer for 5 to 10 minutes. Remove and discard the bay leaf. Serve over hot steamed rice.

Serves 6

Cajun cuisine is best identified by its use of one-pot cooking. In the recipe, the meat, vegetables, and starch are slowly simmered together to create yet another hearty Cajun delicacy.

Natchitoches Meat Pies

Filling
2 1/2 pounds ground beef
2 1/2 pounds ground pork
3 large onions, chopped
3 bell peppers, chopped
1/2 cup minced garlic
4 cups chicken broth or beef broth
3/4 cup all-purpose flour
1 cup chopped green onions
Creole seasoning to taste
Salt and pepper to taste

Pastry
4 cups self-rising flour
1/2 cup shortening
1 cup milk
2 eggs, lightly beaten
1 egg
1 tablespoon water
Vegetable oil for frying

To prepare the filling, brown the beef and pork with the onions, bell peppers and garlic in a large cast-iron skillet. Simmer for 2 hours, adding the broth one cup at a time, once the previous addition has been absorbed. Stir in the flour and green onions. Simmer for 30 minutes. Season with the Creole seasoning, salt and pepper. Remove from the heat and let stand to cool.

To prepare the pastry, process the flour and shortening in a food processor until the mixture resembles cornmeal. Combine the flour mixture, milk and 2 eggs in a mixing bowl. Mix by hand until a soft dough forms. Roll out to 1/8 inch thick on a lightly floured surface. Cut with a 6-inch pastry cutter. Beat 1 egg and the water together in a bowl until smooth. Brush the edges of the pastry circles with the egg wash. Spoon 1 tablespoon of the meat mixture into the center of each pastry circle. Fold one side over the filling making a half-moon shape. Crimp the edges together with a fork. Fry in a deep fryer at 350 degrees until golden brown. Drain on paper towels.

Makes 1 1/2 dozen

The original Louisiana meat pie is believed to have been developed by Natchitoches Indians and improved upon by the Spanish. The current version certainly bears a strong resemblance to Spanish empanadas.

Boudin Blanc

10 pounds Boston butt roast, chopped
2 pounds pork liver, chopped
1 pound green onions
1 pound parsley
6 pounds cooked white rice
8 cups cold water
1 cup chopped pimentos
$^{1}/_{2}$ cup salt
6 tablespoons cayenne pepper
$^{1}/_{4}$ cup black pepper
75 feet sausage casing

Grind the roast, pork liver, green onions and parsley alternately in a meat grinder and combine all in a large mixing bowl. Add the rice, water, pimentos, salt, cayenne pepper and black pepper. Mix well by hand. Cook a small portion of the mixture in a small skillet until cooked through. Adjust the seasonings to the mixture as needed.

Fill the casing using a sausage stuffer, twisting into 6-inch links. Steam for 45 minutes or until the sausage is firm. Serve hot for breakfast or cold as a Cajun canapé.

Makes 125 sausages

Boudin blanc, the Cajun pork and rice sausage, is without a doubt the best-known sausage in south Louisiana. The use of rice and extra spice make Louisiana boudin much different from those of France. Boudin is a delicious by-product of boucheries, and it is well worth the extra effort.

Creole Cream Cheese Strawberry Shortcakes

Strawberries
1 quart strawberries, sliced
$1/2$ cup sugar, or to taste
1 ounce strawberry wine

Creole Cream Cheese
11 ounces Creole cream cheese,
   softened
2 cups heavy whipping cream
$1/2$ teaspoon ground nutmeg
$1/2$ teaspoon cinnamon
$3/4$ cup sugar

Shortcake Biscuits
2 cups all-purpose flour
1 tablespoon baking powder
3 tablespoons sugar, or to taste
$1/2$ teaspoon salt
$11/2$ cups heavy whipping cream
Milk

To prepare the strawberries and creole cream cheese, mix the strawberries, $1/2$ cup sugar and the wine in a bowl. Mash lightly with a fork or potato masher; set aside. Combine the cream cheese, 2 cups cream, the nutmeg and cinnamon in a mixing bowl. Beat on medium-high speed until combined and slightly thickened. Add $3/4$ cup sugar gradually, beating constantly until very soft peaks form. Chill until needed.

To prepare the shortcake biscuits, sift the flour, baking powder, 3 tablespoons sugar and the salt together. Add $11/2$ cups cream gradually, stirring constantly until a soft dough forms. Roll or pat out to $1/2$ inch thick on a lightly floured surface. Cut with a $21/2$-inch biscuit cutter and place on an ungreased baking sheet. Reroll and cut the remaining dough until all is used. Brush the dough with milk. Bake at 425 degrees for 15 minutes or until golden brown. Cool on a wire rack for 5 minutes. Cut the shortbreads into halves horizontally using a fork and place the bottom portion on a dessert plate. Layer with the strawberry mixture and the cream cheese mixture. Replace the tops of the shortbreads.

Makes 10

*P*rime hunting season and strawberry planting season begin about the same time in Louisiana. When the strawberries are ripe, trucks selling the sweet berries line the roads. Here, the fresh produce is combined with Creole cream cheese to create a famous and loved strawberry dish.

Appetizers, Snacks & Beverages

Spa Day

"When I called a friend to request recipes for the St. Vincent de Paul cookbook, she invited me to go along to a Spa Day that a group of young women from her church was putting on at the Sweet Dreams Shelter.

"That Saturday the shelter was alive with sounds of happy chaos. The children who lived in the shelter and the volunteers' children were running around, playing, and sharing the cookies and chips that the volunteers had brought. While the children were occupied, the volunteers gave manicures, pedicures, and back rubs to the women who lived in the shelter.

"I saw a young volunteer kneeling in front of a shelter guest, a woman whose missing teeth and rough, uneven complexion made it plain that hers had not been an easy life. After her pedicure—the first she had ever had—the woman from the shelter was absolutely delighted. Her feet were soft and pretty, but it was her smile that was truly beautiful.

"Before the volunteers left, they gave each woman in the shelter a small manicure kit with a simple prayer tied to the bag.

"All this took place shortly after Holy Week, so the symbolism of Spa Day soon became obvious to me: just as Jesus washed the feet of His disciples, these volunteers were washing the feet of their sisters. And by doing so, they were doing more than making the shelter residents' hands and feet look pretty—they were lifting their sisters up, serving them, ministering to them, just as Jesus showed His disciples and us how we should minister to each other.

"Spa Day at the Sweet Dreams Shelter made it clear to me that this service, this simple but intimate kindness performed by Jesus two thousand years earlier, still has the power to lift up and refresh us. Seeing that young woman kneeling at the feet of a complete stranger brought home to me Christ's command that we serve one another."

Shelter Volunteer

Crawfish Cheesecake

1 cup (4 ounces) grated
   Parmesan cheese
1 cup fresh bread crumbs
1/2 cup (1 stick) butter, melted
1 tablespoon olive oil
1 cup chopped onion
1/2 cup chopped green bell pepper
1/2 cup chopped red bell pepper
1 pound crawfish tails, chopped
2 teaspoons minced garlic

2 tablespoons lemon juice
1 to 2 teaspoons Creole seasoning
1/4 to 1/2 teaspoons Tabasco sauce
2 dashes of Worcestershire sauce
28 ounces cream cheese, softened
4 eggs
1/2 cup heavy cream
1 cup shredded smoked
   Gouda cheese

Mix the Parmesan cheese, bread crumbs and butter in a bowl. Press over the bottom of a 9-inch springform pan. Heat the olive oil in a skillet over medium-high heat. Add the onion, green bell pepper and red bell pepper and sauté for 2 minutes. Add the crawfish, garlic, lemon juice, Creole seasoning, hot sauce and Worcestershire sauce. Sauté for 15 minutes. Remove from the heat.

Beat the cream cheese and eggs in a mixing bowl for 5 minutes or until thick and frothy. Add the crawfish mixture, cream and Gouda cheese. Beat for 2 minutes or until creamy. Pour over the bread crumbs. Bake at 350 degrees for 1 hour or until the center is firm. Cool in the pan. Run a sharp knife around the edge of the cheesecake and remove the side of the pan. Serve with crackers or pita bread. This may be made 1 day in advance and chilled, covered, until serving time.

Serves 12

In keeping with the Louisiana custom of giving "something extra," or as we call it, lagniappe, the footnotes to the recipes contain famous quotations, inspirational sayings, informative facts, or scripture readings intended to nourish the soul. Enjoy!

Layered Crab Dip

8 ounces cream cheese, softened
1 1/2 to 2 tablespoons Worcestershire
   sauce
1 tablespoon minced onion
1 1/2 teaspoons lemon juice
1/2 teaspoon Tabasco sauce
1/2 cup seafood cocktail sauce

8 ounces lump crab meat
4 ounces mozzarella cheese, shredded
2 Roma tomatoes, chopped
2 green onions, chopped
3 to 4 tablespoons grated
   Parmesan cheese

Mix the cream cheese, Worcestershire sauce, onion, lemon juice and hot sauce together in a bowl until creamy. Spread onto a 9- to 10-inch serving platter. Chill, covered, for 4 to 6 hours. Layer with the cocktail sauce, crab meat, mozzarella cheese, tomatoes, green onions and Parmesan cheese. Let stand for 30 minutes before serving. Serve with crackers. For a variation, substitute 12 ounces chopped boiled shrimp for the crab meat.

Serves 6 to 8

Shrimp Butter

8 ounces cream cheese, softened
1/2 cup (1 stick) butter, softened
3 tablespoons mayonnaise
2 cups cooked and peeled shrimp,
   minced (about 1 pound)
1/4 cup fresh parsley, chopped
3 tablespoons grated onion

1 tablespoon lemon juice
1 teaspoon prepared horseradish
1 teaspoon Worcestershire sauce
1 teaspoon Tabasco sauce
1/2 teaspoon red pepper
1/2 teaspoon garlic powder

Process the cream cheese, butter and mayonnaise in a food processor until smooth and creamy. Add the shrimp, parsley, onion, lemon juice, horseradish, Worcestershire sauce, hot sauce, red pepper and garlic powder. Process until combined. Shape the mixture into a ball. Chill, covered, for 4 to 10 hours or until firm. Serve with stone-ground wheat crackers, party rye bread or on toasted bagels.

Serves 4 to 6

Shrimp Nachos

Homemade Salsa
1 (14- or 16-ounce) can
    whole tomatoes
Juice of 1/2 lemon or lime
4 dashes of Tabasco sauce
1 small onion, cut into quarters
1 garlic clove
1/2 cup packed cilantro leaves
Salt to taste

Guacamole
5 Hass avocados, chopped
4 plum tomatoes, seeded
    and chopped
1 onion, chopped
2 cloves garlic, finely chopped
1 jalapeño chile, seeded and chopped,
    or Tabasco sauce to taste

Juice of 1 lime
Dollop of sour cream
1 1/2 teaspoons salt, or to taste
Freshly ground pepper to taste

Assembly
1 (16-ounce) can spicy refried beans
1 (9-ounce) bag extra-thick
    tortilla chips
8 to 12 ounces cooked shrimp,
    coarsely chopped
1 cup (4 ounces) shredded Monterey
    Jack cheese
1 cup (4 ounces) shredded
    Cheddar cheese
2 to 4 pickled jalapeño chiles, sliced
Chopped fresh cilantro
1 cup sour cream

To prepare the salsa, process the tomatoes, lemon juice, hot sauce, onion, garlic and cilantro in a food processor until combined. Season with salt. Chill, covered, for 8 to 10 hours.

To prepare the guacamole, combine the avocados, tomatoes, onion, garlic, jalapeño chile, lime juice, sour cream, salt and pepper in a bowl. Mash or stir until combined. Combine in a food processor and process until smooth, if desired.

To assemble, spread about 1 teaspoon refried beans on each chip. Arrange the chips overlapping slightly on a large round ovenproof platter. Layer with the shrimp, Monterey Jack cheese, Cheddar cheese and jalapeño chiles. Bake at 350 degrees for 8 to 10 minutes or until the cheese is melted. Drizzle with the salsa and sprinkle with cilantro. Store-bought salsa may be substituted for the homemade salsa. Serve immediately with the sour cream and the guacamole on the side.

Serves 6

Miniature Muffulettas

8 ounces pitted green olives, chopped
4 to 5 ounces pitted black
  olives, chopped
3/4 cup finely chopped celery
3 tablespoons finely chopped
  red onion
1/4 cup olive oil
4 teaspoons red wine vinegar
1 teaspoon dried oregano

1 teaspoon garlic powder
1/2 teaspoon pepper
12 Kaiser rolls
12 thin slices smoked ham (8 ounces)
12 thin slices provolone cheese
  (8 ounces)
12 thin slices Genoa salami
  (8 ounces)

Mix the green olives, black olives, celery, onion, olive oil, vinegar, oregano, garlic powder and pepper in a bowl. Slice the rolls into halves horizontally. Spread each bottom half with 2 to 3 tablespoons of the olive mixture. Layer with one slice ham, one slice cheese and one slice salami. Replace the tops of the rolls and place on a rimmed baking sheet. Bake at 325 degrees for 15 minutes or until the cheese begins to melt. Slice each into fourths. Serve warm.

Serves 24

The muffuletta, an Italian-style sandwich, originated in New Orleans, Louisiana, in 1906. They were a creation of Salvatore Lupo at the Central Grocery in the French Quarter and are still being sold there today.

Pepperoni Pinwheels

3½ ounces pepperoni, minced
8 ounces cream cheese, softened
1 cup (4 ounces) shredded
   Cheddar cheese
½ cup sliced black olives
2 tablespoons sliced green onion

2 tablespoons chopped fresh oregano,
   or 2 teaspoons dried oregano
½ teaspoon garlic powder
4 (10-inch) flour tortillas
Salsa

Mix the pepperoni, cream cheese, Cheddar cheese, olives, green onion, oregano and garlic powder in a bowl. Spread about ½ cup of the pepperoni mixture on each tortilla. Roll tightly as for a jelly roll and wrap tightly with plastic wrap. Chill for 2 hours. Unwrap and slice each tortilla into twelve slices. Serve with salsa on the side.

Makes 48

Shelter Scramble Squares

10 ounces frozen chopped broccoli,
   thawed and drained
1 (8-ounce) can whole kernel
   corn, drained
¼ cup chopped onion
½ cup walnuts, coarsely chopped
½ cup milk
¼ cup (½ stick) butter, melted

2 eggs
½ cup baking mix
½ to 1 teaspoon Tabasco sauce
¼ teaspoon garlic salt
Pepper to taste
1 cup (4 ounces) shredded
   Cheddar cheese

Mix the broccoli, corn, onion and walnuts together in a bowl. Pour into a greased 9×9-inch baking dish. Combine the milk, butter, eggs, baking mix, hot sauce, garlic salt and pepper in a mixing bowl. Beat for 1 minute at high speed. Pour over the broccoli mixture. Bake at 375 degrees for 23 to 25 minutes or until a knife inserted into the center comes out clean. Sprinkle with the cheese and bake until the cheese is melted. Let cool in the pan for 30 minutes. Cut into squares.

Makes 30

Zucchini Squares

3 cups thinly sliced zucchini
1 cup baking mix
1 cup (4 ounces) shredded Swiss
   cheese
$1/2$ cup (2 ounces) grated Parmesan
   cheese
$1/2$ cup finely chopped onion
$1/2$ cup vegetable oil

4 eggs, lightly beaten
1 garlic clove, minced
2 tablespoons chopped fresh parsley
$1/4$ teaspoon dried oregano
$1/4$ teaspoon pepper
$1/2$ teaspoon seasoned salt
Salt to taste
Grated Parmesan cheese

Mix the zucchini, baking mix, Swiss cheese, Parmesan cheese, onion, oil, eggs, garlic, parsley, oregano, pepper, seasoned salt and salt in a bowl. Pour into a greased and floured 9×13-inch baking dish. Sprinkle with additional Parmesan cheese. Bake at 350 degrees for 25 to 30 minutes or until light brown. Cut into squares. Serve warm or at room temperature.

Serves 12

As the earth brings forth its plants, and a garden makes its growth spring up, So will the Lord GOD make justice and praise spring up before all the nations.

Isaiah 61:11

42

Sun-Dried Tomato and Pesto Torta

4 garlic cloves
1 1/2 cups packed basil leaves
1/4 cup pine nuts, toasted
2 tablespoons extra-virgin olive oil
1 teaspoon fresh lemon juice
1 1/3 cups drained oil-pack
   sun-dried tomatoes

1/3 cup tomato paste
18 ounces (about) cream
   cheese, softened
3/4 cup (1 1/2 sticks) butter, softened
Salt and pepper to taste
1/4 cup (1 ounce) freshly grated
   Parmesan cheese

Chop the garlic in a food processor. Add the basil, pine nuts, olive oil and lemon juice. Process until chopped and combined. Scrape into a bowl.

Chop the sun-dried tomatoes in the food processor. Add the tomato paste and process until almost smooth. Add 2 ounces of the cream cheese and process until smooth.

Beat the remaining 16 ounces cream cheese and the butter in a mixing bowl until fluffy. Season with salt and pepper. Spray a 6-inch soufflé dish with nonstick cooking spray and line with plastic wrap extending over the side of the dish. Layer 3/4 cup cream cheese mixture, one-half of the tomato mixture, 1/2 cup cream cheese mixture, one-half of the pesto, 1/2 cup cream cheese mixture, the remaining tomato mixture, 1/2 cup cream cheese mixture, the remaining pesto and the remaining cream cheese mixture in the prepared dish. Fold the excess plastic wrap over the cream cheese mixture, covering well. Chill for 8 to 10 hours. This may be prepared up to 3 days in advance.

To serve, unwrap the excess plastic wrap and invert onto a serving platter. Remove the plastic wrap. Garnish with fresh basil sprigs and toasted pine nuts. Serve with toasted baguette slices.

Serves 8 to 10

You loved justice and hated wickedness; therefore God, your God, anointed you with the oil of gladness above your companions.

Hebrews 1:9

Chocolate Chip Cheese Ball

8 ounces cream cheese, softened
1/2 cup (1 stick) butter, softened
1/4 teaspoon vanilla extract
3/4 cup confectioners' sugar

2 tablespoons brown sugar
3/4 cup miniature semisweet
    chocolate chips
3/4 cup finely chopped pecans

Beat the cream cheese, butter and vanilla in a mixing bowl until fluffy. Add the confectioners' sugar and brown sugar gradually, beating constantly. Stir in the chocolate chips. Chill, covered, for 2 hours. Shape the mixture into a ball. Chill, covered, for 1 hour or until serving time. Roll in the pecans and place on a serving platter. Serve with chocolate graham crackers.

Serves 16

Make it a practice to judge persons and things in the most favorable light at all times and under all circumstances.

Saint Vincent de Paul

Blue Cheese Dip

1/2 cup sour cream
4 ounces blue cheese, crumbled
3 ounces cream cheese, softened
1/8 teaspoon hot red pepper sauce

2 tablespoons diced onion
4 slices bacon, crisp-cooked and
    crumbled

Process the sour cream, blue cheese, cream cheese, hot sauce and onion in a blender or food processor until combined, scraping down the side once. Stir in one-half of the bacon and pour into a serving dish. Chill, covered, for 2 hours. Sprinkle with the remaining bacon just before serving. Serve with crackers, fresh vegetables or potato chips.

Makes 1 1/2 cups

Whoever eats without giving thanks steals from God.

Old Jewish Saying

Black Bean and Feta Dip

1 (15-ounce) can black beans,
   drained and rinsed
1 (15-ounce) can white Shoe Peg
   corn, drained
4 green onions, chopped
1/3 cup apple cider vinegar

1/3 cup olive oil
1/3 cup sugar
Dash of garlic powder
Dash of salt
Dash of pepper
4 ounces feta cheese, crumbled

Mix the beans, corn and green onions in a bowl. Whisk the vinegar, olive oil, sugar, garlic powder, salt and pepper in a bowl until blended. Pour over the bean mixture and toss to mix. Chill, covered, for 4 to 10 hours, tossing occasionally. Fold in the cheese just before serving. Serve with corn chips.

Serves 16

Roasted Red Pepper Pesto

1 (12-ounce) jar roasted red bell
   peppers, drained
1/2 cup fresh cilantro leaves, chopped
3 garlic cloves, minced
1 tablespoon tomato paste
1 tablespoon sherry vinegar or white
   wine vinegar

2 teaspoons lemon juice
1 1/4 teaspoons kosher salt
3/4 teaspoon paprika
3/4 teaspoon chili powder
1/4 to 1/2 teaspoon cayenne pepper
1 cup coarsely chopped blanched
   almonds

Process the peppers, cilantro, garlic, tomato paste, vinegar, lemon juice, salt, paprika, chili powder and cayenne pepper in a food processor until the peppers and cilantro are finely chopped. Scrape down the side of the container and process until smooth. Add the almonds and pulse until the almonds are chopped no larger than the size of peppercorns. Serve with crusty bread, crackers or vegetables. Substitute for pizza sauce, mix with cream cheese and serve on toasted bagels, or mix with mayonnaise and use as a sandwich spread or on burgers. This may be chilled, covered, for up to 2 days.

Makes 2 1/2 cups

Olive Dip

1 (10-ounce) jar pimento-stuffed
   green olives
8 ounces cream cheese, softened

1/2 cup mayonnaise
1/2 cup pecans, chopped

Drain the olives, reserving 3 tablespoons of the juice. Chop the olives fine. Mix the cream cheese, mayonnaise and reserved olive juice in a bowl until smooth. Stir in the olives and pecans. Chill, covered, for 8 to 10 hours. Serve with crackers, melba toast or use as a sandwich spread.

Makes 2 1/2 cups

The kindly man will be blessed, for he gives of his sustenance to the poor.

Proverbs 22:9

Tapenade

8 ounces black olives, drained and
   pitted
4 anchovy fillets, rinsed and drained
1/2 cup capers, drained
4 garlic cloves

1/4 teaspoon cayenne pepper
1/4 teaspoon grated orange zest
Leaves of 8 sprigs of thyme
4 to 6 tablespoons olive oil

Pulse the olives, anchovy fillets, capers, garlic, cayenne pepper, orange zest and thyme in a food processor until blended. Add the olive oil 1 tablespoon at a time, pulsing after each addition. Pulse until a coarse paste forms. Serve with toasted French bread slices, on pizza, on vegetable sandwiches or with grilled fresh tuna or beef.

Makes 1 1/4 cups

Jesus said to them, "My food is to do the will of Him who sent me and to finish His work."

John 4:34

Caponatina

1/4 cup olive oil
1 eggplant, peeled and chopped
Salt and pepper to taste
2 tablespoons olive oil
1 small onion, finely chopped
2 to 4 garlic cloves, minced
2 tablespoons olive oil
1 cup finely chopped celery
2/3 cup water

3 ounces tomato paste
3 tablespoons red wine vinegar
1 tablespoon sugar
1/2 teaspoon salt
1/4 teaspoon ground red pepper, or
 to taste
1/2 cup sliced green olives
1 tablespoon drained capers

Heat 1/4 cup olive oil in a large deep skillet over medium-high heat. Add the eggplant and sauté for 12 to 15 minutes or until tender. Season with salt and pepper. Remove the eggplant to a dish. Add 2 tablespoons olive oil, the onion and garlic to the skillet. Season with salt and pepper. Sauté for 4 minutes or until tender and golden brown. Remove the onion and garlic to a dish. Add 2 tablespoons olive oil and the celery to the skillet. Season with salt and pepper. Sauté for 3 minutes or until tender. Remove the celery to a dish.

Combine the water, tomato paste, vinegar, sugar, 1/2 teaspoon salt and the red pepper to the hot skillet. Bring to a boil. Reduce the heat to low and simmer for 10 minutes, stirring frequently. Add the olives and capers and simmer for 3 to 5 minutes. Add the eggplant, onion, garlic and celery. Simmer, covered, for 20 minutes, stirring occasionally. Remove to a serving platter and serve with toasted French bread. This dish is great served cold. Prepare 1 to 2 days in advance. Chill, covered, until serving time.

Serves 6 to 8

He had them ride triumphant over the summits of the land and live off the products of the fields, giving them honey to suck from the rocks and olive oil from its hard, stony ground.

Deuteronomy 32:13

Baguettes Rockefeller

1 cup chopped frozen spinach
2 baguettes
4 green onions, chopped
1/4 cup packed fresh parsley
1/2 cup (1 stick) butter, melted
2 teaspoons anchovy paste
1/2 teaspoon Tabasco sauce

2 teaspoons Pernod, or 1 teaspoon
  anise extract
1/2 teaspoon dried thyme
1/4 teaspoon salt
1/2 cup Italian-style bread crumbs
1 cup (4 ounces) shredded
  Parmesan cheese

Cook the spinach according to the package directions; drain, squeezing out any excess moisture. Slice the bread into 1/2-inch-thick slices and arrange on a baking sheet. Process the spinach, green onions, parsley, butter, anchovy paste, hot sauce, Pernod, thyme and salt in a food processor until combined. Stir in the bread crumbs. Spread about 2 tablespoons of the spinach mixture over each slice of bread. Sprinkle each with about 1/2 teaspoon cheese. Bake at 350 degrees for 15 to 20 minutes or until light brown.

Makes 24

He who cannot cut the bread evenly, cannot get along with people.

Czechoslovakian Proverb

Kahlúa Grapes

1 cup sour cream
1/2 cup packed brown sugar

2 tablespoons Kahlúa
2 pounds seedless green grapes

Mix the sour cream, brown sugar and Kahlúa in a bowl. Stir in the grapes. Chill, covered, for 8 to 10 hours.

Serves 10 to 12

You shall not pick your vineyard bare, nor gather up the grapes that have fallen. These things you shall leave for the poor.

Leviticus 19:10

Spicy Bloody Mary Mix

2 (48-ounce) cans tomato juice
1 (10-ounce) can beef broth
1/2 cup Worcestershire sauce
1/2 cup lemon juice
2 tablespoons prepared horseradish

1 tablespoon seasoned salt
2 teaspoons instant minced onion
2 teaspoons celery seeds
2 teaspoons Creole seasoning
Vodka, to taste (optional)

Combine the tomato juice, broth, Worcestershire sauce, lemon juice, horseradish, seasoned salt, instant minced onion, celery seeds and Creole seasoning in a pitcher. Chill until serving time. Stir in the vodka. Serve with celery sticks or seasoned green beans for special occasions.

Serves 15

Let your speech always be gracious, seasoned with salt, so that you know how you should respond to each one.

Colossians 4:6

Peach Spritzers

3 cups peach purée (about 5 to 6 large peaches)
1 (750-milliliter) bottle Champagne, chilled
1 (23-ounce) bottle sparkling mineral water

Mix the peach purée, Champagne and mineral water in a large pitcher. Pour into chilled wine glasses and serve immediately.

Serves 8 to 10

From the fruit of his words a man eats good things, but the treacherous one craves violence.

Proverbs 13:2

Wedding Punch

4 cups sugar
13 cups water
2 (48-ounce) cans pineapple juice
3 (3-ounce) packages lemon gelatin
   or strawberry gelatin

$2^1/3$ cups powdered lemonade mix
1 (1-ounce) bottle almond extract
3 (750-milliliter) bottles
   Champagne, chilled
1 (3-liter) bottle club soda, chilled

Dissolve the sugar in 4 cups of the water in a saucepan over medium-low heat. Combine the remaining 9 cups water, the pineapple juice, gelatin, lemonade mix and almond extract in a large saucepan. Dissolve the lemonade mix and gelatin over medium-heat. Stir in the sugar water. Let stand until cool. Pour into three $1/2$-gallon freezer-safe containers with tight-fitting lids. Freeze until serving time. Let stand at room temperature until slushy. Mix the lemonade mixture, Champagne and club soda in a punch bowl. For a nonalcoholic version, substitute three chilled 2-liter bottles of lemon-lime soda for the Champagne and club soda. For small groups, mix $1/2$ gallon of the frozen lemonade mixture at a time.

Serves 75

Blessed are those who have been called to the wedding feast of the Lamb.

Revelations 19:9

4-4-4 Fruit Punch

4 cups chilled apple juice
4 cups chilled pineapple juice
4 cups chilled orange juice

2 liters chilled ginger ale
1 quart pineapple sherbet
1 quart orange sherbet

Combine the apple juice, pineapple juice and orange juice in a large punch bowl. Stir gently to mix. Stir in the ginger ale. Spoon small scoops of the pineapple sherbet and orange sherbet into the punch bowl. Serve immediately.

Serves 40 to 45

The earth has yielded its fruits; God our God has blessed us.

Psalms 67:7

Bayou Blue Tea

16 ounces frozen blueberries
1/2 cup fresh lemon juice
4 cups water

3 family-size tea bags
3/4 cup sugar, or to taste

Combine the blueberries and lemon juice in a 2-quart saucepan. Bring to boil over medium-high heat. Cook for 5 minutes, stirring occasionally. Press through a fine wire strainer into a bowl with the back of a spoon. Discard the solids in the strainer. Wipe the saucepan clean. Bring the water to a boil in the saucepan. Remove from the heat and add the tea bags. Let steep for 5 minutes. Remove and discard the tea bags. Stir in the blueberry mixture and sugar. Pour into a pitcher. Chill, covered, until serving time. Serve over ice in tall glasses.

Makes 5 cups

The darker the berry, the sweeter the juice.

American Saying

White Chocolate Latte

2 cups milk
1 cup half-and-half
2/3 cup white chocolate chips
2 tablespoons instant coffee granules

1 teaspoon vanilla extract
1/4 teaspoon almond extract
Sugar to taste (optional)
Whipped cream

Combine the milk, half-and-half, white chocolate chips and coffee granules in a saucepan. Cook over low heat until the chocolate is melted and the mixture is smooth, stirring frequently. Remove from the heat and stir in the flavorings. Ladle into mugs and sweeten. Top with whipped cream or garnish with cinnamon sticks. Serve immediately.

Serves 4

Who has never tasted what is bitter does not know what is sweet.

German Proverb

Double Irish Coffee

6 ounces hot freshly brewed
    strong coffee
1 teaspoon sugar (optional)
2 tablespoons Irish whiskey

2 tablespoons Irish cream liqueur
Whipped cream
Baking cocoa

Pour the coffee into a stemmed glass mug. Stir in the sugar, whiskey and liqueur.
Top with whipped cream. Dust with baking cocoa.

Serves 1

The cream always rises to the top.

American Saying

Café au Lait with a Punch

8 cups brewed strong New Orleans
    blend coffee with chicory, chilled
8 cups milk
1/2 cup crème de cacao or coffee-
    flavored liqueur

3 quarts good-quality vanilla
    ice cream
Whipped cream
Baking cocoa

Combine the coffee, milk and liqueur in a punch bowl. Add 2 quarts of the ice cream
and stir until the ice cream is melted. Place scoopfuls of the remaining 1 quart ice cream
in the punch bowl. Ladle into demitasse cups. Top with dollops of whipped cream and
dust with baking cocoa. Serve immediately.

Serves 30

*Café au lait is a French term that means "coffee on milk." To make traditional café au
lait, milk is scalded and poured into the cup simultaneously with freshly brewed strong
coffee. Thus, the resulting drink is thoroughly mixed.*

Soups, Salads & Breads

ANSWERING PRAYERS

A St. Vincent de Paul Conference is composed of volunteers who go out two by two, just as Jesus sent his disciples out, to visit the poor in their homes. Whether assistance is needed for rent or a broken refrigerator, the volunteers begin by making a home visit. They begin every visit with a prayer, putting any material aid that might be given in the context of Christ and his message of love and social responsibility.

The following story is based on the experience of someone who was helped by a local St. Vincent de Paul Conference.

"It's really hard to ask for help when you're used to taking care of yourself and your children. But after my husband died and I lost my job, I found out that there are people who will help you without making you feel embarrassed.

"I had to move to a one-bedroom apartment, but had no beds. My sister-in-law had given me a couch, and I put my babies to sleep there. Every night I spread a blanket on the floor and slept beside them. One day when I was at a St. Vincent de Paul Thrift Store looking for clothes for my kids, I saw a bed and asked the store manager if I could get it and pay it out over two pay periods. She told me, no, they really didn't do that, but that I could contact the St. Vincent de Paul Conference in my area to get a voucher that would pay for the bed.

"I called the church and left my name and number, explaining my situation and my concern for my babies. There are a lot of really needy people out there, so I didn't know if I would ever hear back, but every day I prayed for God to send me some kind of help.

"A day or two later, while I was praying, there was a knock at the door, and I knew right then that God had answered my prayer. Two people from St. Vincent de Paul were there to help me. They invited me to pray with them. They didn't talk down to me, and I guess that's why I didn't feel embarrassed, like I thought I would. They said, 'Everybody needs help now and then. This just happens to be your time.'

"I have found a better job, and I'm slowly getting the things my family needs. We all have beds now, but I haven't forgotten the kindness of the people from St. Vincent or the time when I slept alongside my babies."

A client helped by a St. Vincent de Paul conference

Father Jeff's Corn and Crab Meat Bisque

6 boiled crabs
2 onions, cut into quarters
3 ribs celery, coarsely chopped
1 bell pepper, cut into quarters
1/2 cup white wine
10 cups water
2 tablespoons Creole seasoning
1/2 cup (1 stick) butter

1 cup chopped yellow onion
3 tablespoons all-purpose flour
1 (12-ounce) can evaporated milk
2 (12-ounce) cans whole kernel corn
1 (8-ounce) can cream-style corn
1/2 teaspoon dried tarragon
1/2 teaspoon liquid crab boil
1/2 cup chopped fresh parsley

Pick the crabs and set the meat aside. Combine the crab shells, 2 quartered onions, the celery, bell pepper and wine in a large heavy saucepan or stockpot. Stir in the water and bring to a boil. Reduce the heat and simmer for 45 minutes. Strain the cooking liquid into a saucepan and keep warm. Remove the shells from the solids and discard. Process the vegetables in a food processor until smooth; set aside. Wipe the saucepan clean.

Melt the butter in the saucepan over medium heat. Stir in 1 cup chopped onion, the flour and evaporated milk and bring to a simmer. Simmer until the onion is translucent, stirring frequently. Stir in the puréed vegetables, 8 cups of the reserved hot crab stock, the undrained whole kernel corn, cream-style corn, tarragon and liquid crab boil. Cook over low heat for 20 minutes, stirring frequently. Stir in the reserved crab meat and the parsley 10 minutes before serving time. Serve with a side salad and toasted French bread, if desired.

Serves 8 to 10

"The Trinity", is a Cajun vegetable combination using equal parts onion, celery and bell pepper. It is most commonly used to flavor soups, stews, and sauces. Its French counterpart, known as Mirepoix, is made with equal parts onion, celery, and carrots.

Crawfish Boil Chowder

1/2 cup (1 stick) butter
1/2 cup all-purpose flour
4 cups half-and-half
1 to 2 cups chicken broth, vegetable broth or seafood stock
1 cup (4 ounces) shredded Cheddar cheese
1/2 cup (2 ounces) shredded Provolone cheese
2 cups crawfish tails
4 cups chopped mixed vegetables
Salt and pepper to taste

Melt the butter in a large saucepan over medium-high heat. Add the flour gradually, stirring constantly until smooth. Add the half-and-half gradually, stirring constantly until thick. Stir in enough of the broth to reach the desired consistency. Add the Cheddar cheese and Provolone cheese. Stir until the cheeses are melted and combined. Add the crawfish tails and mixed vegetables. Reduce the heat to medium-low and simmer until the vegetables are tender. Season with salt and pepper.

Use peeled crawfish tails and vegetables left over from a crawfish boil. The mixed vegetables can include potatoes, corn, mushrooms, onions, carrots and/or garlic. The crawfish and vegetables will be seasoned; taste before adding additional seasonings.

Serves 6

The first record of a commercial crawfish harvest in the United States was in 1880 from the Atchafalaya Basin in Louisiana. That year, a harvest of 23,000 pounds of crawfish was recorded with a value of $2,140.

Commander's Palace Turtle Soup au Sherry

1 cup (2 sticks) unsalted butter
3/4 cup all-purpose flour
1 pound turtle meat, cut into
   1/2-inch pieces
1/4 cup (1/2 stick) unsalted butter
2 onions, minced
1 cup minced celery (about 4 ribs)
11/2 teaspoons minced garlic
3 bay leaves
1 teaspoon oregano

1/2 teaspoon thyme
Salt to taste
1/2 teaspoon pepper
11/2 cups tomato purée
4 cups beef stock
1/2 cup lemon juice
5 hard-cooked eggs, finely chopped
Minced parsley to taste
2 tablespoons dry sherry

Melt 1 cup butter in a saucepan over medium heat. Add the flour and cook until light brown, stirring constantly; set aside. Brown the turtle meat in 1/4 cup butter in a saucepan over high heat. Add the onions, celery, garlic, bay leaves, oregano, thyme, salt and 1/2 teaspoon pepper. Cook until the onions are translucent, stirring frequently. Stir in the tomato purée and reduce the heat. Simmer for 10 minutes. Stir in the stock and simmer for 30 minutes. Add the flour mixture and cook over low heat until smooth and coats the back of a spoon, stirring constantly. Stir in the lemon juice, eggs and parsley. Adjust the seasonings to taste.

Ladle into bowls and spoon 1 teaspoon of the sherry over each serving.

Serves 6

Since 1880, Commander's Palace has been a New Orleans landmark known for the award-winning quality of its food and service. Commander's Palace is brimming with the Brennan family's gracious Crescent City hospitality.

Rainy Day Chicken Soup

1 cup water
2 dried porcini mushrooms
2 tablespoons butter or olive oil
2 boneless skinless chicken breasts
2 leek bulbs, chopped
1 onion, chopped
1 carrot, chopped

1 rib celery, chopped
2 tablespoons all-purpose flour
2 tablespoons dry white wine
4 cups chicken broth
1 cup fat-free sour cream
1 cup fine egg noodles
Salt and pepper to taste

Bring the water to a boil in a saucepan over medium-high heat. Add the mushrooms. Cook for 10 minutes or until tender; drain. Pat the mushrooms dry and thinly slice.

Melt the butter in a large saucepan over low heat. Stir in the chicken, leeks, onion, carrot and celery. Cook, covered, for 10 minutes or until the chicken is cooked through, stirring once. Remove the chicken to a cutting board, reserving the vegetables in the saucepan. Chop the chicken into bite-size pieces.

Stir the flour into the vegetables and cook for 2 minutes, stirring constantly. Add the wine and 2 cups of the broth gradually, stirring constantly until thick and bubbly. Stir in the sour cream gradually.

Bring the remaining 2 cups broth to a boil in a saucepan. Add the noodles and boil for 4 minutes or until almost tender. Stir the noodles with broth, chicken and mushrooms into the vegetable mixture. Simmer over low heat until the chicken is heated through. Season with salt and pepper. Ladle into bowls.

Serves 4

So faith, hope, love remain, these three; but the greatest of these is love.

1 Corinthians 13:13

Hamburger Soup

1 pound lean ground beef
1 large onion, chopped
1 or 2 (14- or 16-ounce) cans
   chopped tomatoes
1 (16-ounce) package frozen
   mixed vegetables
2 ribs celery, chopped

2 carrots, chopped
4 to 5 cups low-sodium chicken broth
1 tablespoon chili powder
Salt and pepper to taste
2 cups rotini, cooked and drained
1/2 cup (2 ounces) grated
   Parmesan cheese

Brown the ground beef in a large heavy saucepan over medium-high heat, stirring until crumbly; drain. Add the onion and cook for 5 minutes, stirring occasionally. Stir in the tomatoes, mixed vegetables, celery, carrots, broth and chili powder. Season with salt and pepper. Bring to a boil and reduce the heat to medium. Simmer until the vegetables are tender. Adjust seasonings to taste. Divide the pasta among serving bowls. Ladle the soup over the pasta and top with the cheese.

Serves 6 to 8

Taco Soup

1 1/2 pounds lean ground beef
1 onion, chopped
1 envelope taco seasoning mix
1 envelope ranch salad dressing mix
1 cup (or more) water
2 (15-ounce) cans pinto beans
1 (15-ounce) can red kidney beans

1 (15-ounce) can whole kernel corn
1 (10-ounce) can Rotel chopped
   tomatoes with green chiles
1 (15-ounce) can stewed tomatoes
1 cup (4 ounces) shredded
   Cheddar cheese

Brown the ground beef with the onion in a large heavy saucepan over medium-high heat, stirring constantly until the ground beef is crumbly and the onion is translucent; drain. Stir in the taco seasoning mix, ranch salad dressing mix and 1 cup water. Stir in the pinto beans, undrained kidney beans, corn, tomatoes with green chiles and stewed tomatoes and bring to a boil. Reduce the heat to medium-low and simmer for 30 minutes. Add additional water if needed. Reduce the heat to low and simmer for 10 minutes. Ladle into bowls and top with the cheese. Serve with corn bread, crackers or corn chips.

Serves 6 to 8

Mushroom Artichoke Soup

1 pound baby portobello
   mushrooms, sliced
1 pound shiitake mushrooms, stems
   removed and caps sliced
1 cup thinly sliced shallots
2 large carrots, peeled and sliced
2 garlic cloves, minced
1/4 cup (1/2 stick) butter
3 tablespoons all-purpose flour
1/2 teaspoon dried thyme

1/4 teaspoon cayenne pepper
28 ounces vegetable broth
2 (14-ounce) cans artichoke hearts,
   drained and quartered
1/4 cup oil-pack sun-dried tomatoes,
   drained and chopped
1 bay leaf
Salt and pepper to taste
1 cup half-and-half
Finely chopped green onions

Sauté the portobello mushrooms, shiitake mushrooms, shallots, carrots and garlic in the butter in a 6-quart heavy saucepan for 15 minutes or until the mushrooms are tender. Stir in the flour, thyme and cayenne pepper. Add the broth gradually, stirring constantly. Cook until slightly thick and bubbly. Stir in the artichoke hearts, sun-dried tomatoes and bay leaf. Season with salt and pepper. Simmer, covered, for 15 minutes, stirring occasionally. Reduce the heat to low and stir in the half-and-half. Remove and discard the bay leaf. Sprinkle with green onions.

Serves 10

Tomato Basil Bisque

2 1/2 cups buttermilk
1 (14-ounce) can chopped tomatoes
   or garlic and oregano chopped
   tomatoes

2 (10-ounce) cans tomato soup
2 teaspoons dried basil
1/4 teaspoon salt
1/4 teaspoon pepper

Combine the buttermilk, tomatoes, soup, basil, salt and pepper in a 3-quart saucepan. Cook over medium heat for 6 to 8 minutes or until heated through. Serve immediately. Serve with grilled cheese sandwiches and fresh fruit, if desired.

Serves 6

Crawfish Pasta Salad

Dressing
3/4 cup canola oil
1/4 cup white balsamic vinegar
2 tablespoons minced garlic
1 tablespoon fresh lemon juice
1 tablespoon chopped fresh parsley
1/2 cup sour cream
1/2 cup nonfat yogurt
1 tablespoon sugar
1 teaspoon dry mustard
2 teaspoons salt
1 teaspoon dried dill weed
1 teaspoon cayenne pepper
1/2 teaspoon black pepper

Salad
16 ounces small pasta shells, cooked
    and drained
1 pint grape tomatoes
1 cup frozen peas, thawed
3/4 cup finely chopped celery
1/2 cup finely chopped orange
    bell pepper
1/2 cup finely chopped yellow
    bell pepper
1/2 cup finely chopped green onions
1 pound cooked peeled crawfish tails

To prepare the dressing, whisk the canola oil, vinegar, garlic, lemon juice and parsley in a bowl until blended. Whisk in the sour cream, yogurt, sugar, dry mustard, salt, dill weed, cayenne pepper and black pepper. Chill until needed.

To prepare the salad, combine the pasta, tomatoes, peas, celery, orange bell pepper, yellow bell pepper and green onions in a large serving bowl. Toss to mix. Add the crawfish and the dressing. Toss to coat. Chill, covered, for 6 to 10 hours.

Serves 6 to 8

Simon Peter went over and dragged the net ashore full of one hundred fifty-three large fish. Even though there were so many, the net was not torn.

John 21:11

Crawfish Remoulade Salad

1/2 cup light mayonnaise
1/2 cup plain nonfat yogurt
3 green onions, minced
4 garlic cloves, minced
2 tablespoons Creole mustard
1 tablespoon chopped fresh parsley

1/2 teaspoon ground red pepper
Salt to taste
2 teaspoons olive oil
1 pound crawfish tails
1 to 1 1/2 heads romaine,
    finely chopped

Mix the mayonnaise and yogurt in a bowl until smooth. Stir in the green onions, garlic, Creole mustard, parsley, red pepper and salt. Heat the olive oil in a skillet over medium-high heat. Add the crawfish and cook for 3 minutes or until cooked through, stirring frequently. Let cool completely. Stir into the mayonnaise mixture. Chill, covered, for 6 to 8 hours. Serve over the lettuce. Shrimp or crab meat may be substituted for the crawfish.

Serves 4 to 6

Chicken Salad

4 pounds chicken tenders
Salt, black pepper and cayenne
    pepper to taste
14 hard-cooked eggs, peeled

4 cups plus 1 tablespoon
    (about) mayonnaise
2 bunches green onions, finely chopped
4 ribs celery, finely chopped
2 to 4 tablespoons canola oil

Combine the chicken with enough water to cover in large saucepan or stockpot and bring to a boil. Reduce the heat to medium-high and cook for 35 minutes or until cooked through and tender; drain. Let cool completely. Chop in a food processor and place in a large bowl. Season with salt, black pepper and cayenne pepper. Separate the egg whites from the egg yolks. Finely chop the egg whites and add to the chicken. Mash the egg yolks in a bowl. Add 1 to 2 cups mayonnaise and mix well. Stir in the green onions, celery and enough canola oil to moisten the mixture. Add to the chicken mixture and mix well. Add the remaining mayonnaise until of the desired consistency. Season with salt and black pepper. Chill, covered, for 4 to 5 hours. Serve on croissants or use to make party sandwiches.

Serves 20

Bean Salad

2 (15-ounce) cans wax beans, drained
  and rinsed
2 (15-ounce) cans cut green beans,
  drained and rinsed
1 (15-ounce) can French-style green
  beans, drained
4 ribs celery, chopped
2 red onions, sliced into rings
1 green bell pepper, cut into
  1-inch slices

1 (4-ounce) jar pimento, drained
1 cup balsamic vinegar
1/2 cup vegetable oil
3/4 cup sugar
1 tablespoon salt
Dash of ketchup
Pepper to taste
Garlic juice to taste

Combine the wax beans, cut green beans, French-style green beans, celery, onions, bell pepper and pimento in a bowl. Toss to mix. Whisk the vinegar, oil, sugar, salt, ketchup, pepper and garlic juice in a bowl until blended. Pour over the bean mixture and toss to coat. Chill, covered, for 24 hours, stirring gently occasionally. Toss well before serving.

Serves 6 to 8

Southwestern Corn and Black Bean Salad

2 cups frozen whole kernel corn
1/4 cup lime juice
2 tablespoons extra-virgin olive oil
1/4 cup chopped cilantro
1/2 teaspoon salt
Freshly ground pepper to taste
2 cups shredded red cabbage

2 (15-ounce) cans black beans,
  drained and rinsed
1 large tomato, chopped
1/2 cup minced red onion
1 to 2 ounces pine nuts, toasted
Crushed corn chips (optional)

Cook the corn according to the package directions; drain. Whisk the lime juice, olive oil, cilantro, salt and pepper in a bowl until blended. Add the corn, cabbage, beans, tomato, onion and pine nuts. Toss to mix. Chill, covered, for up to 24 hours. Sprinkle with crushed corn chips just before serving.

Serves 6 to 8

Mardi Gras Broccoli Salad

Florets of 1 bunch broccoli
(5 to 6 cups)
1/2 cup chopped red onion
1/2 cup golden raisins
10 slices bacon, crisp-cooked
and chopped

1/2 cup chopped pecans
1 cup mayonnaise
2 tablespoons sugar or sugar
substitute
2 tablespoons cider vinegar

Combine the broccoli, onion, raisins, bacon and pecans in a serving bowl. Toss to mix. Whisk the mayonnaise, sugar and vinegar in a bowl until blended. Pour over the broccoli mixture and toss to mix. Chill, covered, for 4 hours.

Serves 6

Mardi Gras colors are purple for justice, green for faith, and gold for power.

Marinated Carrot Salad

2 pounds baby carrots
1 green bell pepper, seeded and sliced
into rings
1 onion, sliced into rings
1 (10-ounce) can tomato soup
1/2 cup sugar

1/2 cup vinegar
1/2 cup vegetable oil
2 tablespoons ketchup
1 teaspoon salt
1/8 teaspoon pepper

Combine the carrots with enough water to cover in a large saucepan. Bring to a boil and cook, covered, until tender-crisp; drain. Combine the carrots, bell pepper and onion in a bowl. Whisk the soup, sugar, vinegar, oil, ketchup, salt and pepper in a bowl until blended. Pour over the carrot mixture and toss to mix. Chill, covered, until serving time.

Serves 8

A joyful life is an individual creation that cannot be copied from a recipe.

Mihaly Csikszentmihalyo, Psychologist

Olive Pasta Salad

1/4 cup (1 ounce) grated
    Parmesan cheese
1/4 cup (1 ounce) grated
    Romano cheese
1 cup mayonnaise
1 tablespoon olive oil
1 teaspoon garlic powder

10 ounces pasta shells, cooked
    and drained
1 (12-ounce) jar olive salad
    mix, drained
1 cup frozen peas, thawed
1/4 cup chopped green onions
Salt and pepper to taste

Combine the Parmesan cheese, Romano cheese, mayonnaise, olive oil and garlic powder in a bowl. Mix well. Add the pasta, olive salad mix, peas and green onions. Toss to mix. Season with salt and pepper. Garnish with sliced green olives and sprigs of parsley.

Serves 8 to 10

One must be poor to know the luxury of giving.

George Eliot, English Novelist

Poor Man's Salad

1 pound bacon, crisp-cooked
    and crumbled
1 cup chopped onion

2 large tomatoes, chopped
1/3 cup (about) mayonnaise
Salt and pepper to taste

Combine the tomatoes, onion, and bacon in a bowl. Toss to mix. Stir in enough of the mayonnaise to reach the desired consistency. Season with salt and pepper. Serve on a bed of lettuce, serve with crackers or use as a sandwich spread, in pita pockets or on panini.

Serves 6

Life's prime needs are water, bread, and clothing, a house, too, for decent privacy. Better a poor man's fare under the shadow of one's own roof than sumptuous banquets among strangers.

Sirach 29:21–22

Spinach and Strawberry Salad

3 tablespoons strawberry jelly
3 tablespoons red wine vinegar
1/4 cup canola oil
1 tablespoon poppy seeds
1 teaspoon salt
1 teaspoon dry mustard
1/4 teaspoon paprika

6 ounces spinach leaves
1 cup sliced strawberries
3/4 cup seedless red grapes,
  cut into halves
1/4 red onion, thinly sliced
1/4 cup toasted pecans or honey-
  roasted sliced almonds

Whisk the jelly, vinegar, canola oil, poppy seeds, salt, dry mustard and paprika in a bowl until blended. Add the spinach, strawberries, grapes, onion and pecans. Toss to coat. For a variation, substitute or add other fruits, such as blueberries and kiwifruit.

Serves 6 to 8

Frozen Cranberry Salad

8 ounces cream cheese, softened
2 tablespoons sour cream
2 tablespoons sugar
1 (16-ounce) can whole berry
  cranberry sauce

1 (20-ounce) can crushed
  pineapple, drained
1/2 cup chopped pecans or walnuts
8 ounces whipped topping
Lettuce leaves

Mix the cream cheese, sour cream and sugar in a bowl until smooth. Stir in the cranberry sauce and pineapple. Fold in the pecans and whipped topping. Pour into an 8×8-inch pan and freeze, covered, until firm. Let stand at room temperature for 30 minutes. Cut into squares and serve slightly frozen over lettuce leaves. Garnish with sweetened dried cranberries.

Serves 9

See, I give you every seed-bearing plant all over the earth and every tree that has seed-bearing fruit on it to be your food; and all the animals of the land, all the birds of the air, and all the living creatures that crawl on the ground, I give you all the green plants for food.

Genesis 1:29-30

Fruity Coleslaw

1 (16-ounce) package coleslaw mix
1 (20-ounce) can pineapple
    chunks or pineapple
    tidbits, drained
1 (15-ounce) package raisins or
    sweetened dried cranberries

1 pound seedless red grapes,
    cut into halves
2 ounces chopped pecans or
    slivered almonds
8 ounces whipped topping
2 tablespoons mayonnaise

Combine the coleslaw mix, pineapple, raisins, grapes and pecans in a serving bowl. Combine the whipped topping and mayonnaise in a small bowl and mix well. Add to the coleslaw mixture and toss to mix. Chill for 4 to 5 hours.

Serves 20

Patience is bitter but its fruit is sweet.

French Proverb

Easy Fruit Salad

1 (21-ounce) can peach pie filling
1 (20-ounce) can pineapple
    chunks, drained
1 (15-ounce) can mandarin
    oranges, drained

1 (10-ounce) package frozen
    strawberries, thawed and drained
4 bananas, sliced

Place the pie filling in a bowl. Fold in the pineapple, oranges, strawberries and bananas. Chill, covered, for 4 to 5 hours.

Serves 8 to 10

From the fruit of his mouth a man has his fill; with the yield of his lips he sates himself.

Proverbs 18:20

Crawfish Corn Bread

Vegetable oil
1 cup cornmeal
1¹/2 teaspoons salt
¹/2 teaspoon baking soda
3 eggs
3 tablespoons (or more) vegetable oil

1 (15-ounce) can cream-style corn
1 pound crawfish tails, rinsed
    and drained
1 small onion, chopped
¹/4 cup finely chopped jalapeño chiles
8 ounces shredded Cheddar cheese

Add enough oil to a heavy cast-iron skillet to cover the bottom of the skillet. Heat in a 375-degree oven. Do not let the oil burn. Mix the cornmeal, salt and baking soda together. Beat the eggs in a large bowl. Stir in 3 tablespoons oil, the corn, crawfish, onion, jalapeño chiles and cheese. Add the dry ingredients and mix well. Pour into the hot skillet. Bake at 375 degrees for 55 minutes or until golden brown. Let stand for 10 minutes before slicing. Serve warm.

Serves 8

The universal brotherhood of man is our most precious possession.

Mark Twain

Jalapeño Corn Bread

1 tablespoon vegetable oil
1¹/3 cups cornmeal
1 tablespoon baking powder
1 teaspoon salt
1 cup cream-style corn
1 cup sour cream
2 eggs, lightly beaten

¹/3 cup vegetable oil
2 jalapeño chiles, seeded
    and chopped
¹/4 cup chopped bell pepper
¹/4 cup chopped onion
1 cup (4 ounces) shredded
    Cheddar cheese

Add 1 tablespoon oil to an 8×8-inch baking pan and heat in a 375-degree oven. Mix the cornmeal, baking powder and salt in a bowl. Add the creamed corn, sour cream, eggs and ¹/3 cup oil and mix well. Stir in the remaining ingredients. Pour into the hot pan. Bake at 425 degrees for 25 minutes. Let stand for 5 minutes before slicing.

Serves 9

Italian Olive Bread

1 (4-ounce) can black olives, chopped
1/2 cup drained pimento-stuffed
   green olives
2 garlic cloves, minced
3/4 cup (3 ounces) shredded Colby
   Jack cheese

1/2 cup (2 ounces) grated
   Parmesan cheese
1/4 cup (1/2 stick) butter, melted
1 tablespoon olive oil
2 to 5 drops of hot red pepper sauce
1 1/2 loaves prepared garlic bread

Process the black olives, green olives, garlic, Colby Jack cheese, Parmesan cheese, butter, olive oil and hot sauce in a food processor until combined. Spread the cut sides of the garlic bread with the olive mixture. Place on baking sheets. Bake at 350 degrees for 15 minutes or until bubbly. Slice 1 to 2 inches thick.

Serves 10 to 20

Asphodel Bread

5 cups Pioneer biscuit and
   baking mix
1/4 cup sugar
1/2 teaspoon salt

2 cups milk
2 envelopes dry yeast
4 eggs
1/4 teaspoon cream of tartar

Sift the baking mix, sugar and salt together into a large bowl. Heat the milk to about 110 degrees in a saucepan. Remove from the heat. Sprinkle the yeast over the warm milk and let stand for 5 minutes to soften. Stir until the yeast is dissolved. Beat the eggs and cream of tartar in a bowl until combined. Stir in the yeast mixture. Add to the dry ingredients and mix well. The dough will be heavy and sticky. Cover and let rise in a warm place until doubled in bulk. Punch the dough down. Let rise until doubled in bulk. Divide the dough into three greased 4×8-inch loaf pans. Bake at 350 degrees for 30 minutes. This bread freezes well after baking.

Makes 3 loaves

Asphodel Plantation in East Feliciana Parish was established in the 1820s and was named after the Greek word for daffodil. A restaurant was opened on the property in the 1960s and Asphodel Bread was a signature dish.

Upside-Down French Toast

1/2 cup (1 stick) butter
1 cup packed brown sugar
1 tablespoon light corn syrup
1/2 cup coarsely chopped pecans
6 eggs, beaten
11/2 cups milk

2 teaspoons granulated sugar
1 teaspoon cinnamon
1 teaspoon vanilla extract
1 (12-ounce) loaf day-old French
   bread, cut into 1-inch slices
1/2 cup coarsely chopped pecans

Combine the butter, brown sugar and corn syrup in a saucepan. Cook over low heat until the mixture is thick and begins to bubble, stirring frequently. Spread over the bottom of a 9×13-inch baking dish. Sprinkle with 1/2 cup pecans.

Combine the eggs, milk, granulated sugar, cinnamon and vanilla in a shallow dish and mix well. Add the bread in batches and soak until soft, turning once. Arrange the bread in a single layer over the pecans. Pour any remaining egg mixture over the bread. Sprinkle with 1/2 cup pecans. Chill, covered, for 8 to 10 hours. Bake, uncovered, at 350 degrees for 35 to 40 minutes. Serve warm.

Serves 6 to 8

Pumpkin Bread

31/2 cups all-purpose flour
2 cups sugar
2 teaspoons baking soda
11/2 teaspoons salt
1 teaspoon cinnamon
1/2 teaspoon ground nutmeg

1/4 teaspoon ground cloves
4 eggs
2 cups canned pumpkin
1 cup vegetable oil
2/3 cup buttermilk

Combine the flour, sugar, baking soda, salt, cinnamon, nutmeg and cloves together. Beat the eggs in a large bowl with a fork until foamy. Stir in the pumpkin, oil and buttermilk. Add the dry ingredients and mix well. Divide among two 5×8-inch loaf pans sprayed with nonstick cooking spray. Bake at 325 degrees for 1 hour or until the loaves test done. Cool in the loaf pans for 10 minutes. Remove to a wire rack to cool completely.

Serves 20

Main Courses

Not Your Everyday Dining Room

Every year, our St. Vincent de Paul Dining Room serves more than 200,000 meals to the poor, homeless, and elderly. But we don't serve numbers—we serve people. And every one has a story. We couldn't resist sharing this one with you.

"One day while I was serving in our dining room, I noticed a family come through the door. The mother, father, and three children stopped just inside the door and looked around.

"The father approached me and asked how much we charged for lunch. He explained that they had been traveling by bus for several days. Now they were out of money, and the sandwiches they had made for their trip were long gone. He was having trouble getting in touch with a relative in the area, and someone at the bus station had told him about St. Vincent de Paul. The family had walked several blocks, the father lugging a suitcase and carrying the youngest child. I could see how weary he was, but his main concern was for his children, who hadn't eaten a hot meal in days.

"I explained to him that our meals were free and they were welcome to join us for lunch. I watched as the children ate their beef stew and wiped the last bit of gravy from their plates. When I walked over to take them some cookies, the little boy looked up at me and said, 'Ma'am, that was so good. The rice and gravy sent me to heaven.'

"The family stayed at our shelter for the night, where they were able to have baths, change into clean clothes, and eat another good meal. The next day their relative picked them up at our shelter.

"As for me, whenever I cook rice and gravy for the dining room, I think about that family and their little boy. No matter what we're cooking, I make sure it's a little taste of heaven."

St. Vincent de Paul Food Services Director

Bass with Summer Squash

1 large red onion, chopped
1 teaspoon grated lemon zest
1 tablespoon extra-virgin olive oil
8 ounces zucchini, cut into
   1/2-inch pieces
8 ounces yellow squash, cut into
   1/2-inch pieces
2 garlic cloves

Salt and pepper to taste
4 (4- to 6-ounce) bass fillets
1 tablespoon extra-virgin olive oil
1 tablespoon red wine vinegar
1 tablespoon water
2 tablespoons finely chopped
   mint leaves

Combine the onion, reserving 1 tablespoon, the lemon zest and 1 tablespoon olive oil in a bowl. Toss to mix. Spread onto a rimmed baking sheet. Bake at 400 degrees for 15 minutes or until the onion is tender, stirring occasionally. Add the zucchini, yellow squash and garlic. Season with salt and pepper. Toss to mix. Bake for 10 minutes. Remove from the oven. Increase the oven temperature to 450 degrees.

Slide the vegetables to one side of the baking pan. Arrange the fish on the baking pan skin side down and season with salt and pepper. Spoon the vegetables over the fish. Bake for 8 to 15 minutes or until the fish is opaque and begins to flake.

Whisk 1 tablespoon olive oil, the vinegar, water, mint and 1 tablespoon reserved onion in a bowl until blended. Spoon over the vegetables and fish just before serving. Any firm fish may be substituted for the bass.

Serves 4

Jesus came over and took the bread and gave it to them, and in like manner the fish. This was now the third time Jesus was revealed to his disciples after being raised from the dead.

John 21:13-14

Roasted Catfish with Sweet Potatoes and Corn Salad

1 pound sweet potatoes
1 tablespoon canola oil
$1/2$ teaspoon ground cumin
4 (4- to 6-ounce) catfish fillets
1 to $1^1/2$ teaspoons chili powder
$1/2$ cup sliced scallions
$2^1/2$ cups frozen corn, thawed

1 bell pepper, seeded and chopped
2 tablespoons fresh lime juice
1 tablespoon chopped fresh cilantro
1 teaspoon finely chopped
   jalapeño chile
Salt and pepper to taste

Peel and slice the sweet potatoes $1/4$ inch thick. Place in a 9×13-inch baking dish. Drizzle with the canola oil and sprinkle with the cumin. Toss to mix and spread out into a single layer. Bake at 400 degrees for 45 minutes or until brown. Remove from the oven and increase the oven temperature to 450 degrees. Turn the sweet potatoes over using a spatula. Arrange the fish over the sweet potatoes. Sprinkle the fish with the chili powder and the scallions. Bake for 8 to 10 minutes or until the fish is opaque and begins to flake.

Combine the corn, bell pepper, lime juice, cilantro and jalapeño chile in a bowl. Season with salt and pepper. Toss to mix.

Remove the fish and sweet potatoes to dinner plates. Serve with the corn salad.

Serves 4

They all ate and were satisfied. And they picked up twelve wicker baskets full of fragments and what was left of the fish. Those who ate of the loaves were five thousand men.

Mark 6:42-44

74

Salmon Steaks with Pecan Butter

Pecan Butter
1/2 cup (1 stick) butter, softened
1/3 cup finely chopped pecans
1 tablespoon chopped fresh flat-leaf
　parsley or fresh chives
1 tablespoon lemon zest
1 teaspoon lemon juice
2 teaspoons freshly grated ginger
1/4 teaspoon salt
1/4 teaspoon ground red pepper

Salmon
4 (6-ounce) salmon steaks
1 tablespoon pecan oil
1 teaspoon salt
1/2 teaspoon black pepper
1/4 teaspoon ground red pepper

To prepare the butter, beat the butter and pecans in a mixing bowl until blended. Add the parsley, lemon zest, lemon juice, ginger, salt and red pepper and mix well.

To prepare the salmon, rub the salmon with the pecan oil. Season with salt, black pepper and red pepper. Place on a grill rack over hot coals and grill for 8 to 10 minutes or until the fish begins to flake, turning once. Remove to a serving platter and top each salmon steak with one or two dollops of the pecan butter. Garnish with fresh parsley and toasted chopped pecans. Serve immediately.

Serves 4

Fish, to taste right, must swim three times—in water, in butter and in wine.

Polish Proverb

Pan-Fried Red Snapper with Artichokes and Mushrooms

1 egg, beaten
1 cup milk
1/2 cup all-purpose flour
4 (10-ounce) red snapper fillets
2 tablespoons butter, melted
Salt and pepper to taste
1 cup vegetable oil
1 (14-ounce) can artichoke hearts,
   drained and cut into quarters

1 cup fresh mushrooms, sliced
1/4 cup (1/2 stick) butter
1 teaspoon Worcestershire sauce
1 teaspoon lemon juice
1 teaspoon tarragon vinegar
1/3 cup sliced almonds, toasted

Mix the egg and milk in a shallow dish until smooth. Place the flour in a separate shallow dish. Brush the fish with 2 tablespoons butter and season with salt and pepper. Dip in the egg mixture and dredge immediately in the flour, shaking off any excess. Heat the oil in a deep heavy skillet over medium-high heat. Fry the fish in the hot oil until golden brown and the fish begins to flake, turning once; drain. Remove to a serving platter and keep warm.

Sauté the artichoke hearts and mushrooms in 1/4 cup butter in a skillet until tender. Stir in the Worcestershire sauce, lemon juice and vinegar. Simmer for 1 minute. Spoon over the fish and sprinkle with the almonds. Serve immediately.

Serves 4

When they climbed out on shore, they saw a charcoal fire with fish on it and bread.

John 21:9

76

Crab Meat Imperial

1 pound lump crab meat
1/4 cup chopped green bell pepper
1/4 cup chopped celery
1 (2-ounce) jar chopped
   pimento, drained
2 tablespoons butter
2 teaspoons chopped fresh parsley

1 teaspoon Old Bay seasoning
1/2 teaspoon butter-flavored salt
1/2 teaspoon prepared mustard
Dash of Tabasco sauce
Dash of red pepper
1 egg, beaten
3 tablespoons mayonnaise

Wash and drain the crab meat. Pick through the crab meat gently, discarding any bits of shell or cartilage; set aside.

Sauté the bell pepper, celery and pimento in the butter in a skillet until tender. Stir in the parsley, Old Bay seasoning, butter-flavored salt, mustard, hot sauce and red pepper.

Mix the egg and mayonnaise in a bowl until smooth. Stir a small portion of the hot vegetable mixture into the egg mixture, and then stir into the remaining vegetable mixture in the skillet. Fold in the crab meat. Divide among four 6-ounce ramekins sprayed with nonstick cooking spray.

Bake at 350 degrees for 15 to 20 minutes. Broil 5 inches from the heat source for 3 minutes or until golden brown. Garnish each with a dollop of additional mayonnaise, two pimento strips and a slice of olive.

Serves 4

From the fruit of his words a man has his fill of good things, and the work of his hands comes back to reward him.

Proverbs 12:14

Crab Meat and Shrimp over Cheese Grits

Cheese Grits
4 cups water
1 teaspoon salt
1 cup grits
1/4 cup (1/2 stick) butter or margarine
1 cup (4 ounces) shredded
   Cheddar cheese
1 teaspoon Worcestershire sauce
2 eggs
1/4 cup milk or cream
Tabasco sauce to taste
Salt to taste

Crab Meat and Shrimp
1/4 cup (1/2 stick) butter
2 tablespoons olive oil

1/3 cup all-purpose flour
2/3 cup chopped onion
1/4 cup chopped green bell pepper
1/4 cup chopped celery
3 garlic cloves, minced
1 (14-ounce) can chicken broth
1/3 cup dry white wine
1/4 cup chopped green onions
1 tablespoon tomato paste
1 tablespoon chopped fresh parsley
1 tablespoon Creole seasoning
2 teaspoons Worcestershire sauce
1/2 teaspoon hot red pepper sauce
4 pounds peeled and deveined
   medium or large shrimp
1 pound crab meat, drained and flaked

To prepare the cheese grits, bring the water and 1 teaspoon salt to a boil in a saucepan. Add the grits gradually, whisking constantly. Cook, covered, according to the package directions. Stir in the butter, cheese and Worcestershire sauce. Beat the eggs in a bowl until frothy. Stir a small portion of the hot grits into the eggs, and then add the eggs to the remaining grits in the saucepan. Stir in the milk. Season with the hot sauce and salt. Pour into a lightly greased 8×8-inch baking dish. Bake at 350 degrees for 25 to 30 minutes.

To prepare the shrimp and crab meat, melt the butter with the olive oil in a large heavy saucepan over medium-high heat. Stir in the flour and cook for 5 minutes or until golden brown, stirring constantly. Add the onion, bell pepper and celery. Cook for 4 minutes or until the vegetables are tender, stirring constantly. Add the garlic and cook for 1 minute, stirring constantly. Stir in the broth, wine, green onions, tomato paste, parsley, Creole seasoning, Worcestershire sauce and hot sauce. Simmer for 10 minutes, stirring occasionally. Stir in the shrimp. Cook, covered, for 5 minutes or until the shrimp turn pink. Fold in the crab meat. Cook until the crab meat is heated though. Serve over the hot cheese grits.

Serves 8

Shrimp Po' Boys

1 (10-ounce) package Louisiana Fish Fry Products seasoned fish fry
1/2 cup water
2 pounds deveined peeled shrimp
Vegetable oil for frying
6 to 8 (6-inch) loaves po' boy bread or soft French bread

Combine 5 tablespoons fish fry and the water in a bowl and mix well. Place the remaining fish fry in a shallow bowl. Dip the shrimp in the batter and dredge immediately in the dry fish fry, coating well and shaking off any excess. Heat the oil in a deep fryer to 350 degrees. Fry the shrimp a few at a time for 3 to 4 minutes or until golden brown. Drain on a paper-towel lined plate.

Slice the bread into halves horizontally. Place equal amounts of the shrimp on the cut side of half of the loaves. Dress with any combination of the following: mayonnaise, mustard, ketchup, cocktail sauce, tartar sauce, rémoulade sauce, hot red pepper sauce, lettuce, tomatoes and pickles. Top with the remaining loaf halves.

Serves 6 to 8

Tony's Seafood traces its roots back to 1959 when Donaldsville, Louisiana, native Tony Pizzolato opened a small wholesale and retail produce business in Baton Rouge. Realizing the locals' love for fresh seafood, Tony added crawfish, shrimp, and crabs to his produce. People come from all over South Louisiana to enjoy Tony's cuisine and to purchase the freshest seafood around and their Louisiana Fish Fry Products.

Shrimp Baton Rouge

1 cup chopped green onions
1 (4-ounce) can sliced mushrooms, drained
$1/2$ cup (1 stick) unsalted butter
$1^1/2$ teaspoons red pepper
1 to $1^1/2$ teaspoons black pepper
1 to $1^1/2$ teaspoons salt
1 teaspoon garlic powder
1 teaspoon paprika
$1/2$ teaspoon onion powder
$1/2$ teaspoon dried oregano
$1/2$ teaspoon dried thyme
1 pound shrimp, peeled
2 cups heavy cream
1 (10-ounce) can cream of mushroom soup
Hot cooked pasta

Sauté the green onions and mushrooms in the butter in a large saucepan over medium-high heat for 4 to 5 minutes or until tender. Stir in the red pepper, black pepper, salt, garlic powder, paprika, onion powder, oregano and thyme. Add the shrimp and cook for 3 to 4 minutes, stirring constantly. Reduce the heat to medium. Stir in the cream and soup. Cook, uncovered, for 20 minutes, stirring occasionally. Serve over hot cooked pasta.

Serves 6 to 8

Baton Rouge was named in 1699 when Iberville led an expedition along the Mississippi River. Diaries of the explorers tell a tale of a pole stained with the blood of fish and animals that served as the dividing line between the Bayougoula and Houmas Indians. It is from the "red stick" that Iberville christened the city "le Baton Rouge."

Blend of the Bayou

1/2 cup (1 stick) butter, chopped
8 ounces cream cheese, chopped
2 pounds peeled crawfish tails
1 cup chopped onion
1 cup chopped green bell pepper
8 ounces mushrooms, sliced
2 tablespoons butter
1 (10-ounce) can cream of
   mushroom soup

2 cups cooked rice
1 tablespoon garlic powder, or
   to taste
1/2 teaspoon red pepper
3 dashes of white pepper
1 1/2 to 2 cups shredded
   processed cheese
1 cup canned French-fried
   onion rings

Combine 1/2 cup butter and the cream cheese in a saucepan. Cook over low heat until melted and smooth, stirring constantly; set aside.

Sauté the crawfish, onion, bell pepper and mushrooms in 2 tablespoons butter in a skillet until the vegetables are tender. Stir in the cream cheese mixture, soup, rice, garlic powder, red pepper and white pepper. Adjust the seasonings to taste. Pour into a greased 9×13-inch baking dish. Top with the processed cheese and onion rings. Bake at 350 degrees for 30 minutes or until bubbly.

This dish may be made 1 day in advance. This dish freezes well. Shrimp or crab meat may be substituted for the crawfish.

Serves 8 to 10

Bayou (pronounced BY-U) is a small secondary river that feeds into larger bodies of water. It is often marshy and slow moving. Louisiana is often referred to as "The Bayou State" because of the many slow, sluggish streams that meander through the lowlands and marshes of the southern section of the state.

Crawfish Pie

1 onion, finely chopped
1 small bunch green onions, finely chopped
1 small green bell pepper, finely chopped
1/3 cup finely chopped celery
1/2 cup (1 stick) butter
1 (10-ounce) can cream of mushroom soup
3 to 4 tablespoons white wine
2 teaspoons Worcestershire sauce
1 teaspoon sugar
1/2 teaspoon salt
1/2 teaspoon black pepper
1/8 teaspoon cayenne pepper
1 pound crawfish tails
1/2 cup seasoned bread crumbs
1 (2-crust) pie pastry
1 tablespoon butter, melted

Sauté the onion, green onions, bell pepper and celery in 1/2 cup butter in a large skillet over medium heat until tender. Stir in the soup, wine, Worcestershire sauce, sugar, salt, black pepper and cayenne pepper. Reduce the heat to low and simmer for 5 to 10 minutes. Stir in the crawfish and simmer for 10 to 15 minutes. Remove from the heat and stir in the bread crumbs.

Fit a 9-inch deep-dish pie plate with one crust. Pour the crawfish mixture into the pastry-lined pie plate. Top with the remaining pastry, crimping or fluting the edge. Cut eight to ten small slits in the top pastry to vent. Brush with 1 tablespoon butter. Bake at 375 degrees for 35 to 45 minutes or until golden brown. Let stand for 10 minutes before slicing.

Serves 6 to 8

Breaux Bridge, Louisiana, is considered the "Crawfish Capital of the World." Crawfish season is from late February to mid-May.

Crawfish in a Bundle

1/4 cup (1/2 stick) butter
1 cup chopped celery
1/2 cup chopped onion
1 teaspoon salt
1 teaspoon lemon pepper
1 teaspoon Creole seasoning
1 pound crawfish tails
1/2 cup pitted black olives, sliced

1/2 cup mayonnaise
1 teaspoon dry mustard
1/2 cup (2 ounces) shredded
  mozzarella cheese
1/2 cup (2 ounces) shredded
  Cheddar cheese
1 (16-ounce) loaf French bread
Melted butter

Melt the butter in a skillet over low heat. Add the celery, onion, salt, lemon pepper and Creole seasoning. Cook for 5 minutes or until the celery and onion are tender, stirring frequently. Stir in the crawfish and olives. Cook for 5 minutes or until the crawfish are cooked through. Stir in the mayonnaise and dry mustard. Remove from the heat and fold in the mozzarella cheese and Cheddar cheese.

Slice the bread into halves horizontally and hollow out the bottom half to make a shell. Discard the removed bread or reserve for another use. Fill the bottom half with the crawfish mixture and replace the top. Brush the outside with butter, if desired. Wrap with foil and place on a baking sheet. Bake at 400 degrees for 30 minutes. Cut into pieces.

The crawfish filling may also be served as an appetizer. Keep hot in a chafing dish and serve with melba toasts.

Serves 6

Many a man curses the rain that falls upon his head, and knows that it brings abundance to drive away hunger.

St. Basil

Crawfish Jambalaya

1/2 cup finely chopped green bell pepper
1/2 cup finely chopped onion
1/2 cup (1 stick) butter
1 (14-ounce) can beef broth
1 (10-ounce) can Rotel chopped tomatoes with green chiles
1 pound crawfish tails
1 (4- to 6-ounce) can sliced mushrooms, drained
1 tablespoon Creole seasoning, or to taste
1 1/2 cups rice

Sauté the bell pepper and onion in the butter in a large heavy saucepan over medium heat until the vegetables are tender. Stir in the broth, tomatoes with green chiles, crawfish, mushrooms and Creole seasoning. Bring to a boil and stir in the rice. Reduce the heat to low and simmer, covered, for 30 minutes or until the liquid is absorbed and the rice is tender. Do not stir while the rice is cooking.

This dish may be made in a rice cooker. Combine all the ingredients in a rice cooker and cook for 30 minutes or until the rice is tender.

Serves 4 to 6

"Jambalaya, a-Crawfish Pie, a-Filé Gumbo," known as the Hank Williams Special in Cajun restaurants, are the beginning lyrics to the song "Jambalaya" performed by Hank Williams, Sr.

Crawfish Étouffée with Basil Biscuits

Basil Biscuits
3 cups baking mix
1 cup milk
1/2 cup (1 stick) butter, melted
1 tablespoon dried basil

Étouffée
1/2 cup (1 stick) butter
1/3 cup all-purpose flour
1 cup chopped onion
1 cup chopped celery
1 cup chopped green bell pepper

2 garlic cloves, minced
1 pound crawfish tails
1 1/2 cups water
1 (8-ounce) can tomato sauce
1/4 cup fresh parsley, chopped
1 teaspoon (heaping) instant
   chicken bouillon
1/2 teaspoon salt
1/8 teaspoon black pepper
1/8 teaspoon ground red pepper
6 to 7 drops of Tabasco sauce

To prepare the biscuits, mix the baking mix, milk, butter and basil in a bowl. Turn out onto a lightly floured surface or pastry cloth and shape into a ball. Knead three to four times. Roll to 1/4 inch thick. Cut with a 2- or 3 1/2-inch biscuit cutter and arrange on a baking sheet. Bake at 450 degrees for 11 to 13 minutes or until light brown.

To prepare the étouffée, melt the butter in 3-quart saucepan over medium-high heat. Stir in the flour and cook until golden brown, stirring constantly. Add the onion, celery, bell pepper and garlic. Cook until the vegetables are tender, stirring constantly. Stir in the crawfish, water, tomato sauce, parsley, bouillon, salt, black pepper, red pepper and hot sauce. Reduce the heat to medium-low and simmer, covered, for 20 minutes. Split the biscuits into halves and place in shallow bowls or on dinner plates. Spoon the étouffée over the biscuits. Serve immediately.

Hot cooked rice may be substituted for the biscuits.

Serves 6 to 8

Étouffée (pronounced ay-too-FAY) comes from the French word étouffer, which means "to smother." It is a spicy and delicious Cajun stew traditionally prepared with crawfish, vegetables, and a dark roux.

Oysters à la Mosca

1 quart medium shucked oysters (about 48)
1 large onion, chopped
3 garlic cloves, finely chopped
1/2 cup (1 stick) butter
2 tablespoons dried parsley
3/4 teaspoon dried oregano
1/2 teaspoon dried thyme
1 teaspoon salt
1/4 teaspoon black pepper
1/4 teaspoon cayenne pepper
1 cup seasoned bread crumbs
1/2 cup (2 ounces) grated Parmesan cheese

Drain the oysters, reserving the liquid. Sauté the onion and garlic in the butter in a skillet for 5 to 6 minutes or until the onion is tender. Stir in the parsley, oregano, thyme, salt, black pepper and cayenne pepper. Add the oysters and cook until the edges begin to curl, stirring frequently. Stir in the reserved oyster liquid and the bread crumbs. Pour into a lightly greased 9×13-inch baking dish. Sprinkle with the cheese. Bake at 350 degrees for 15 to 20 minutes.

Serves 6

Mosca's is a legendary roadside restaurant located near New Orleans. It was opened in 1949 by Provino and Lisa Mosca and is still owned and operated by family members.

African Chicken

1 large onion, chopped
2 garlic cloves, crushed
1/4 cup vegetable oil
3 pounds chicken pieces
1 large bell pepper, chopped
1 pound mushrooms, coarsely chopped
12 ounces tomato sauce
1/4 teaspoon dried oregano
1/4 teaspoon dried thyme
Salt and pepper to taste
1/4 cup chunky peanut butter, or to taste
Hot cooked rice
Chopped peanuts (optional)

Sauté the onion and garlic in the oil in a large skillet until the onion is translucent. Add the chicken and cook until light brown, turning occasionally. Add the bell pepper, mushrooms, tomato sauce, oregano and thyme. Season with salt and pepper. Bring to a boil, stirring occasionally. Reduce the heat and simmer, covered, for 45 minutes, stirring occasionally. Return to a boil and stir in the peanut butter. Serve over hot cooked rice. Sprinkle with chopped peanuts.

Serves 6 to 8

From jazz funerals, to spicy cuisine, to popular musical forms, the African-American presence is an essential ingredient to the cultural gumbo of Louisiana.

Chicken Mole

1 tablespoon cornstarch
1 (10-ounce) can chopped tomatoes
2 pounds boneless skinless
   chicken breasts
2 tablespoons vegetable oil
1/2 cup chopped onion
1 garlic clove, minced
1 teaspoon chili powder

1/8 teaspoon cinnamon
1/8 teaspoon ground cloves
1/4 cup canned chopped green chiles
1 teaspoon salt
1 chicken bouillon cube, crumbled
2 (1.76-ounce) Milky Way Midnight
   candy bars, chopped
Hot cooked rice

Dissolve the cornstarch in the tomatoes in a bowl; set aside. Brown the chicken in the oil in a large skillet over medium heat. Remove the chicken to a shallow 2-quart baking dish, reserving the drippings in the skillet. Add the onion and garlic to the reserved drippings and cook until tender, stirring constantly. Do not brown. Stir in the chili powder, cinnamon and cloves and cook for 1 minute. Stir in the tomato mixture, green chiles, salt, bouillon cube and candy bars. Cook until the candy bars are melted and combined, stirring constantly. Pour over the chicken.

Bake at 325 degrees for 1 hour or until the chicken is cooked through and tender, basting with the pan juices three to four times during cooking. Let stand for 5 minutes. Remove the chicken to a serving platter. Skim the pan gravy. Spoon the gravy over the chicken. Serve over hot cooked rice.

Serves 4 to 6

Put falsehood and lying far from me, give me neither poverty nor riches; provide me only with the food I need.

Proverbs 30:8

Sherried Artichoke Chicken

8 chicken breasts
1 teaspoon salt
$1/2$ teaspoon paprika
$1/4$ teaspoon pepper
$1/4$ cup olive oil or margarine
1 (14-ounce) can artichoke hearts,
    drained and cut into quarters

2 tablespoons olive oil or margarine
4 ounces mushrooms, sliced
2 tablespoons flour
1 (14-ounce) can chicken broth
3 tablespoons sherry

Season both sides of the chicken with the salt, paprika and pepper. Brown in $1/4$ cup hot olive oil in a skillet over medium-high heat. Remove the chicken to a 9×13-inch baking dish sprayed with nonstick cooking spray, reserving the drippings in the skillet. Arrange the artichoke hearts over the chicken.

Add 2 tablespoons olive oil and the mushrooms to the reserved drippings. Cook until the mushrooms are tender, stirring frequently. Add the flour and cook for 1 minute, stirring constantly. Stir in the broth and sherry. Reduce the heat to low and simmer for 5 minutes. Pour over the artichoke hearts. Bake, covered with foil, at 375 degrees for 1 hour. Let stand for 5 minutes before serving.

Serves 8

Hot Chicken Salad

2 cups chopped cooked chicken
2 cups chopped celery
1 cup mayonnaise
$1/2$ cup slivered blanched almonds
2 tablespoons fresh lemon juice

$1/2$ teaspoon grated onion
$1/2$ teaspoon salt
$2/3$ cup crushed potato chips
$1/2$ cup (2 ounces) grated
    Cheddar cheese

Mix the chicken, celery, mayonnaise, almonds, lemon juice, onion and salt in a bowl. Spoon into a 2-quart baking dish. Mix the potato chips and cheese in a bowl. Sprinkle over the chicken mixture. Bake, uncovered, at 375 degrees for 20 minutes or until heated through. This dish is great served for a luncheon with sliced fruit and croissants.

Serves 6

Chicken Supreme

1 (6-ounce) package long grain and
   wild rice with herbs
3¹/2 cups chopped cooked chicken
1 cup finely chopped sweet onion
1 (14-ounce) can French-style green
   beans, drained
1 (10-ounce) can cream of celery soup

1 (4-ounce) jar chopped
   pimentos, drained
1 cup chopped water
   chestnuts, drained
1/2 cup mayonnaise
Salt and pepper to taste

Cook the rice according to the package directions; drain. Combine the chicken, onion, beans, soup, pimentos, water chestnuts and mayonnaise in a bowl and mix well. Fold in the rice. Season with salt and pepper. Spoon into a lightly greased 9×13-inch baking dish. Bake at 350 degrees for 45 minutes. Let stand for 5 minutes before serving.

Serves 6 to 8

Quail with Mushroom Gravy

6 quail, cut into halves
Salt and pepper to taste
1/2 cup (1 stick) butter
3 tablespoons all-purpose flour

8 ounces mushrooms, sliced
2 cups chicken broth
1/2 cup pale dry sherry
Hot cooked rice

Spray the quail with nonstick cooking spray and season with salt and pepper. Brown the quail in the butter in a large skillet over medium-high heat. Remove the quail skin side up to a 9×13-inch baking dish, reserving the drippings in the skillet. Stir the flour into the drippings. Reduce the heat to medium-low and stir in the mushrooms, broth and sherry. Simmer until heated through. Pour over the quail. Bake at 350 degrees for 1 hour. Serve over hot cooked rice.

Serves 6

Louisiana is also known as "Sportsman's Paradise." This nickname pays tribute to the wildlife and the hunting, trapping, and fishing resources of the state, as well as other outdoor recreational and sporting activities within the state.

Fried Turkey

1 (10- to 14-pound) turkey
1 (14-ounce) can chicken broth
3 ounces garlic juice
1/4 cup Tabasco sauce
3 tablespoons Worcestershire sauce
1 tablespoon salt
1 teaspoon cayenne pepper
25 bay leaves, finely ground

3 tablespoons Creole seasoning
1 tablespoon dried thyme, ground
1 tablespoon dried oregano, ground
2 teaspoons garlic powder
1 1/2 teaspoons black
   peppercorns, ground
4 to 5 gallons peanut oil

To determine the oil level needed, place the turkey in the turkey fryer pot and cover with enough water to cover by 2 inches. Remove the turkey and measure the water level. Discard the water and thoroughly clean and dry the fryer pot.

Wash the turkey inside and out under cold water and pat dry. Mix the broth, garlic juice, hot sauce, Worcestershire sauce, salt and cayenne pepper in a bowl. Fill a meat injector with the broth mixture. Inject the meaty parts of the turkey. Mix the bay leaves, Creole seasoning, thyme, oregano, garlic powder and peppercorns in a bowl. Divide into three portions. Rub one portion inside the turkey. Rub one portion under the skin over the breasts. Do not tear the skin. Rub the remaining portion over all of the skin. Place in a roasting pan. Chill, covered, for up to 24 hours.

Let the turkey stand for 30 minutes or until room temperature. Sew the turkey neck flap securely to the bottom of the turkey. Fold the wings under. Set up the burner outdoors on level ground away from anything flammable. Add enough peanut oil to the fryer pot to reach where the water level was measured. Heat the peanut oil to 325 to 350 degrees. Place the turkey in a fryer basket or on a fryer hanger and submerge slowly into the hot oil. Deep-fry for 30 to 40 minutes or until a meat thermometer inserted into the breast registers 170 degrees. Remove the turkey carefully from the oil and place on a wire rack over a roasting pan. Drain for 15 minutes before serving.

Serves 10

Fried turkey originated in Bayou (Louisiana/Texas) Creole cuisine but is gaining popularity nationwide. Deep-fried turkey is moist and delicious and not at all greasy. It is a tasty alternative to traditional fall holiday roast turkey.

Cider-Glazed Pork Chops with Sweet Potato and Andouille Hash

16 cups apple cider
2 tablespoons butter
4 pounds sweet potatoes, peeled
   and chopped
6 tablespoons extra-virgin olive oil
Salt and pepper to taste
4 links andouille, chopped

1 red onion, chopped
6 garlic cloves, sliced
1 tablespoon cumin
1 tablespoon cinnamon
4 ounces chopped cilantro
3 or 4 (10-ounce) pork chops

Cook the cider in a saucepan over medium-high heat for 1 1/2 hours or until reduced to a thick syrup. Stir in the butter 1 tablespoon at a time, stirring well after each addition. Remove from the heat and set aside.

Arrange the sweet potatoes on a foil-lined baking sheet. Drizzle with the olive oil and season with salt and pepper. Toss to mix. Bake at 350 degrees until tender.

Cook the sausage in saucepan over low heat until crisp. Add the onion and garlic. Cook for 5 minutes, stirring frequently. Add the cumin and cinnamon. Stir in the sweet potatoes. Cook until the sweet potatoes are heated through. Remove from the heat and stir in the cilantro.

Place the pork chops on a grill rack over hot coals and grill until the pork chops are cooked through. Brush with the cider syrup. Slice and remove to a platter. Serve with the sweet potato and andouille hash.

Serves 6 to 8

Character is like a tree and reputation like its shadow. The shadow is what we think of it; the tree is the real thing.

Abraham Lincoln, 16th President of the United States

Pork Chops with Apple Cream Sauce

4 (8-ounce) bone-in center-cut pork
   loin chops
1/2 teaspoon dried thyme
1/2 teaspoon salt
1/4 teaspoon pepper
1 tablespoon olive oil

2 large Vidalia onions
1 1/2 cups apple juice or apple cider
1 1/2 cups low-sodium chicken broth
1/2 cup heavy cream
4 teaspoons Dijon mustard

Season the pork with the thyme, salt and pepper. Heat the olive oil in a large skillet over medium-high heat. Add the pork chops and cook for 8 minutes or until brown, turning once. Remove to a dish, reserving the drippings in the skillet.

Slice the onions into halves and slice each half into 1/4-inch-thick slices. Add to the reserved drippings and cook for 8 minutes or until tender, stirring constantly. Spray with nonstick cooking spray, if needed. Pour 2/3 cup of the apple juice over the onions and arrange the pork chops over the onions. Cook, covered, over medium heat for 15 minutes or until the pork chops are cooked through. Remove the pork chops to a serving platter. Remove the onions with a slotted spoon and arrange over the pork chops, reserving the drippings in the skillet. Keep warm.

Add the remaining apple juice and the broth to the skillet. Cook over high heat for 6 to 8 minutes, stirring frequently. Reduce the heat to medium-low and stir in the cream. Cook for 5 to 10 minutes, stirring frequently. Do not boil. Remove from the heat and stir in the Dijon mustard. Drizzle some of the sauce over the pork chops and serve the remaining sauce on the side. Baked sweet potatoes are a nice accompaniment for this dish.

Serves 4

Then will the desert become an orchard and the orchard be regarded as a forest. Right will dwell in the desert and justice abide in the orchard. Justice will bring about peace; right will produce calm and security.

Isaiah 32:15–17

Creole Pork Chops

1/4 cup all-purpose flour
1/2 teaspoon salt
1/4 teaspoon pepper
1/4 teaspoon dried rosemary, crushed
6 (1/2-inch-thick) deboned
   pork chops
2 tablespoons vegetable oil
1/4 cup (1/2 stick) butter
3/4 cup finely chopped onion
3/4 cup finely chopped green
   bell pepper

2 ribs celery, thinly sliced
2 garlic cloves, minced
2 cups beef broth
8 ounces mushrooms, cut into halves
3 or 4 tomatoes, peeled and cut
   into quarters
1 (6-ounce) can tomato paste
1 tablespoon chopped fresh parsley
1 bay leaf
1/4 to 1/2 teaspoon Creole seasoning
3 cups hot cooked rice

Mix the flour, salt, pepper and rosemary in a shallow dish. Dredge the pork chops in the flour mixture, shaking off any excess. Brown the pork chops in the oil in a skillet over medium heat. Remove to a 9×13-inch baking dish sprayed with nonstick cooking spray, reserving the drippings in the skillet.

Add the butter, onion, bell pepper, celery and garlic to the reserved drippings and cook until the vegetables are tender, stirring constantly. Stir in the broth, mushrooms, tomatoes, tomato paste, parsley, bay leaf and Creole seasoning. Simmer, uncovered, for 20 minutes, stirring occasionally. Remove and discard the bay leaf. Pour the sauce over the pork chops. Bake, covered, at 325 degrees, for 1 hour or until the pork chops are cooked through and tender. Serve over the rice.

Serves 6

If your enemy is hungry, give him something to eat; if he is thirsty, give him something to drink.

Proverbs 25:21

Helenihi Pork Loin

2 tablespoons soy sauce
2 tablespoons peanut butter
1/2 to 1 teaspoon crushed red
    pepper flakes

2 garlic cloves, minced
1 pound pork loin
1/4 cup pineapple preserves
1/4 cup water

Mix the soy sauce, peanut butter, red pepper flakes and garlic in a bowl. Spread over the pork and place in a small roasting pan. Bake at 350 degrees for 30 minutes. Spread the preserves over the pork. Bake for 15 minutes longer. Remove the pork to a carving board, reserving the drippings in the pan. Let stand for 10 minutes before slicing. Stir the water into the reserved drippings. Pour into a sauce bowl and serve with the pork.

Serves 4

Pork Medallions Louisianne

12 (1/2-inch-thick) boneless
    pork medallions
Salt and black pepper to taste
Cayenne pepper to taste
1/4 cup olive oil
1 bunch of green onions (white parts
    only), chopped

1 tablespoon chopped garlic
1 cup dry white wine
1/4 cup cane syrup
4 ounces Demi-Glace (page 28)
    or prepared brown gravy
1/2 cup chopped pecans, toasted

Season the pork with salt, black pepper and cayenne pepper. Heat the olive oil in a skillet over medium-high heat. Add the pork and cook until cooked through, turning occasionally. Remove to a serving platter and keep warm, reserving the drippings in the pan. Add the green onions and garlic to the reserved drippings and sauté until tender. Add the wine and cook, stirring constantly and scraping up any brown bits from the bottom of the skillet. Reduce the heat to medium-low and simmer for 10 minutes. Strain through a fine wire sieve into a saucepan. Discard the solids. Return to the heat and reduce the liquid by one-half. Stir in the cane syrup, Demi-Glace and pecans, reserving a few pecans for garnish. Simmer until thick. Ladle over the pork and garnish with the reserved pecans. Serve warm.

Serves 6

Dry-Rubbed Baby Back Ribs

1/4 cup paprika
1 1/2 tablespoons brown sugar
1 1/2 tablespoons freshly ground
   black pepper
1 tablespoon salt
1 1/2 teaspoons celery salt

1 1/2 teaspoons cayenne pepper
1 1/2 teaspoons ground cumin
1 1/2 teaspoons garlic powder
1 1/2 teaspoons dry mustard
4 to 6 pounds baby back pork ribs
Mop sauce or barbecue sauce

Mix the paprika, brown sugar, black pepper, salt, celery salt, cayenne pepper, cumin, garlic powder and dry mustard in a bowl. Trim the thin membrane from the ribs. Rub two-thirds of the spice rub over both sides of the ribs and place in dish. Chill, covered, for 4 to 8 hours. Place on a grill rack and grill over medium heat for 1 hour. Baste with mop sauce and continue to grill for 30 to 60 minutes or until the meat comes away from the ends of the bones. Sprinkle with the remaining spice rub 15 minutes before the end of cooking.

Serves 6

Italian Sausage and Pepper Pasta

16 ounces penne
1 1/4 pounds hot Italian sausage,
   casings removed
1 (6-ounce) jar roasted red bell
   peppers, drained and chopped
1 large sweet onion, chopped

1 green bell pepper, chopped
1 tablespoon minced garlic
1 (15-ounce) can chopped tomatoes
   with onions, garlic and olive oil
1/2 cup (2 ounces) grated
   Parmesan cheese

Cook the pasta according to the package directions; drain. Brown the sausage in a large skillet, stirring constantly until crumbly. Remove with a slotted spoon to paper towel-lined plates to drain, reserving the drippings in the skillet. Add the onion, roasted red bell peppers, green bell pepper and garlic to the reserved drippings and cook for 8 to 10 minutes or until the vegetables are tender, stirring constantly. Stir in the sausage and tomatoes. Simmer for 15 minutes. Serve over the hot pasta. Sprinkle with the cheese.

Serves 4 to 6

Garlic White Lasagna

1¹/2 pounds hot Italian sausage, casings removed
1 onion, chopped
4 large garlic cloves, minced
1 (12-ounce) jar roasted red bell peppers, drained and chopped
¹/2 cup Chardonnay or other dry white wine
1 (10-ounce) package frozen chopped spinach

15 ounces ricotta cheese
1 egg, lightly beaten
¹/2 teaspoon salt
¹/2 teaspoon pepper
2 (17-ounce) jars Alfredo sauce
12 no-boil lasagna noodles
12 ounces sliced mozzarella cheese
1 cup (4 ounces) grated or finely shredded Parmesan cheese

Brown the sausage in a skillet over medium heat, stirring until crumbly. Drain, reserving 1 tablespoon of the drippings in the skillet. Add the onion and garlic to the reserved drippings. Cook over medium-high heat until the onion is tender, stirring constantly. Stir in the sausage, red bell peppers and wine. Bring to a boil. Reduce the heat and simmer, uncovered, for 5 minutes or until the liquid is almost evaporated.

Cook the spinach according to the package directions; drain. Combine the spinach, ricotta cheese, egg, salt and pepper in a bowl and mix well.

Layer 1 cup Alfredo sauce, four lasagna noodles, one-half of the spinach mixture, one-half of the sausage mixture and four slices of mozzarella cheese. Continue layering 1 cup Alfredo sauce, four lasagna noodles, the remaining spinach mixture, the remaining sausage mixture, the remaining lasagna noodles, the remaining mozzarella cheese and the remaining Alfredo sauce. Top with the Parmesan cheese. Chill, covered, for 8 to 10 hours, if desired.

Let stand at room temperature for 30 minutes. Bake, covered, at 350 degrees for 45 minutes. Bake, uncovered, for 15 minutes longer. Let stand 15 minutes before slicing.

Serves 8

Jesus said to Peter, "Feed my sheep."
John 21:17(b)

Grecian Skillet Rib-Eye Steaks

1¹/₂ teaspoons dried basil
1¹/₂ teaspoons garlic powder
1¹/₂ teaspoons dried oregano
¹/₂ teaspoon salt
¹/₈ teaspoon pepper
2 (1-inch-thick) beef rib-eye steaks
1 tablespoon olive oil
1 tablespoon fresh lemon juice
2 tablespoons crumbled feta cheese
1 tablespoon chopped black olives

Mix the basil, garlic powder, oregano, salt and pepper in a small bowl. Rub over both sides of the steaks. Heat the olive oil in a large nonstick skillet. Add the steaks and cook for 10 to 14 minutes or until medium-rare, turning once. Sprinkle with the lemon juice and remove to a serving platter. Top with the cheese and olives.

Serves 2 to 4

Blessed be the fruit of your womb, the produce of your soil and the offspring of your livestock, the issue of your herds and the young of your flocks!

Deuteronomy 28:4

Beef Brisket with Barbecue Sauce

Brisket
1 (4-pound) beef brisket
Creole seasoning to taste
Cracked pepper to taste
Garlic powder to taste

Barbecue Sauce
1 small onion, chopped
1/2 green bell pepper, finely chopped

1 garlic clove, minced
1 cup apple cider vinegar
1/2 cup ketchup
2 tablespoons Worcestershire sauce
2 tablespoons brown sugar
1 teaspoon dry mustard
1 teaspoon salt
1/2 teaspoon paprika
1/4 teaspoon pepper

To prepare the brisket, season the brisket with the Creole seasoning, pepper and garlic powder. Place in a roasting pan. Bake, uncovered, at 300 degrees for 4 hours or until tender. Let stand until cool. Remove to a cutting board and slice into thin strips. Return to the roasting pan.

To prepare the sauce, combine the onion, bell pepper and garlic in a saucepan. Stir in the vinegar, ketchup, Worcestershire sauce, brown sugar, dry mustard, salt, paprika and pepper. Bring to a boil and reduce the heat to medium-low. Simmer for 15 minutes. Pour over the sliced brisket. Bake, covered, at 325 degrees for 1 hour.

Serves 6 to 8

Lord, you are the true nourishment of the souls, and he who worthily receives you will be partaker and heir of the eternal glory.

Thomas à Kempis

Corned Beef and Vegetables

Horseradish Sauce

1 cup sour cream
1/2 cup mayonnaise
1/3 cup prepared horseradish, or
  to taste
2 teaspoons lemon juice
Pinch of ground red pepper
Salt and freshly ground black pepper
  to taste

Corned Beef

1 (3- to 31/2-pound) beef brisket with
  spice envelope
15 ounces beef broth
1 teaspoon liquid crab boil
1 pound small red or Yukon gold
  potatoes, cut into halves
8 ounces baby carrots
1 pound Savoy cabbage, cut into
  wedges and cored

To prepare the sauce, combine the sour cream, mayonnaise, horseradish and lemon juice in a bowl and mix well. Season with the ground red pepper, salt and black pepper. Chill, covered, for 1 hour or until serving time.

To prepare the corned beef, arrange the beef brisket fat-side up in a large heavy saucepan. Add the spice envelope, beef broth, crab boil and enough water to cover. Bring to a boil over medium-high heat. Reduce the heat to low. Simmer, covered, for 2 hours 45 minutes or until fork-tender. Remove the beef brisket to a carving board, reserving the liquid in the saucepan.

Skim the surface of the reserved liquid. Add the potatoes and carrots and bring to a boil over medium-high heat. Discard some of the liquid if needed. Reduce the heat to medium-low. Simmer, covered, for 10 minutes. Add the cabbage and cook for 15 minutes or until the vegetables are tender. Drain, discarding the liquid.

Slice the corned beef into thin strips. Serve with the vegetables and horseradish sauce.

Serves 6 to 8

Laughter is brightest in the place where the food is.

Irish Proverb

French Dip Sandwiches

1 (10-ounce) can beef broth
5 1/2 ounces water
1 envelope Italian salad dressing mix
1 envelope au jus gravy mix
1 3/4 teaspoons dried minced onion
1 teaspoon crushed red pepper flakes
3/4 teaspoon salt
1/2 teaspoon dry mustard

1/2 teaspoon dried oregano
1/2 teaspoon paprika
1/8 teaspoon garlic powder
1/8 teaspoon black pepper
1 (4- to 5-pound) sirloin tip
   roast, trimmed
Po' boy bread or soft French bread,
   sliced horizontally

Mix the broth and water in a slow cooker. Stir in the salad dressing mix, gravy mix, dried minced onion, red pepper flakes, salt, dry mustard, oregano, paprika, garlic powder and black pepper. Add the roast. Cook on Medium for 6 to 8 hours or until the roast is fork-tender. Remove the roast to a cutting board, reserving the liquid in the slow cooker. Let cool slightly. Slice across the grain into thin strips. Return to the slow cooker. Serve on slices of bread.

For a variation, toast the bread in the oven. Spread mayonnaise over the cut sides of half the bread slices and top with Provolone cheese. Remove the beef with a slotted spoon and place over the cheese. Top with the remaining bread slices. Serve with a small bowl of the pan juices on the side.

Serves 10 to 12

In 1929, the Martin brothers and former streetcar drivers created an inexpensive sandwich of gravy and spare bits of roast beef on French bread and served it to striking streetcar drivers. When a worker came to get a sandwich, the cry would go up in the kitchen that "here comes another poor boy!," and the name was transferred to the sandwich, eventually becoming "Po' boy" in common usage.

Grillades

4 pounds round steak
All-purpose flour
Salt and pepper to taste
1/4 to 1/2 cup vegetable oil
1 1/2 cups chopped bell peppers
1 cup chopped onion
3/4 cup chopped celery
2 garlic cloves, minced
1/2 cup chopped fresh parsley
1/2 cup all-purpose flour
2 cups chopped tomatoes or canned
   tomatoes, drained

1 cup water
1 cup red wine
2 tablespoons Worcestershire sauce
Tabasco sauce to taste
2/3 teaspoon dried thyme
1/2 teaspoon tarragon (optional)
2 bay leaves
Salt and pepper to taste
3 tablespoons chopped fresh parsley

Slice the beef into 3×3-inch pieces. Season flour with salt and pepper in a shallow bowl. Dredge the beef in the flour mixture, shaking off any excess. Heat 1/4 cup oil in a large skillet over medium-high heat. Brown the beef in batches in the hot oil, adding additional oil as needed. Remove to a dish, reserving the drippings in the skillet.

Add the bell peppers, onion, celery, garlic and 1/2 cup parsley to the reserved drippings, adding additional oil as needed. Cook until the vegetables are tender, stirring occasionally. Stir in 1/2 cup flour. Add the tomatoes, water and wine gradually, stirring constantly. Stir in the Worcestershire sauce, hot sauce, thyme, tarragon and bay leaves. Season with salt and pepper. Add the beef and reduce the heat to medium-low. Simmer, covered, for 1 hour, stirring frequently. Remove and discard the bay leaves. Sprinkle with 3 tablespoons parsley just before serving. This dish may be baked, covered, in a large roasting pan at 200 degrees for 6 hours, if preferred.

Serves 12 to 16

Grillades are a traditional South Louisiana brunch dish and are usually served over plain grits or cheese grits.

Italian Sauce with Meatballs

Meatballs

1 pound lean ground beef
1/2 cup Italian bread crumbs
1/4 cup (1 ounce) grated
    Parmesan cheese
1 to 2 garlic cloves, minced
2 eggs, lightly beaten
1 1/2 tablespoons chopped Italian flat-
    leaf parsley
Salt and pepper to taste
1 to 3 tablespoons water

Italian Sauce

1 large onion, finely chopped
4 garlic cloves, minced
1/4 cup olive oil
2 (6-ounce) cans tomato paste
2 (14-ounce) cans whole tomatoes,
    drained and crushed
5 to 6 cups (or more) water
1 tablespoon sugar
3/4 tablespoon salt
Pepper to taste
1 teaspoon dried oregano
2 basil leaves, chopped
2 bay leaves
Hot cooked pasta

To prepare the meatballs, combine the ground beef, bread crumbs, cheese, garlic, eggs and parsley in a bowl. Season with salt and pepper. Mix by hand until combined. Add the water 1 tablespoon at a time, mixing well after each addition. The mixture should be moist but not fall apart. Shape into balls and place on rack on a broiler pan. Broil until light brown, turning once.

To prepare the sauce, sauté the onion and garlic in the olive oil in a saucepan over medium-high heat until tender. Stir in the tomato paste and reduce the heat to medium. Cook for 15 minutes, stirring constantly. Stir in the tomatoes, water, sugar, salt and pepper. Reduce the heat to medium-low and simmer for 2 1/2 hours, stirring occasionally. Stir in the meatballs, oregano, basil and bay leaves. Simmer for 30 minutes. Stir in boiling water as needed to thin the sauce. Remove and discard the bay leaves. Serve over hot cooked pasta.

Serves 4

Salt is good, but if salt becomes insipid, with what will you restore the flavor? Keep salt in yourselves and you will have peace with one another.

Mark 9:50

Baked Spaghetti

1 1/2 pounds ground beef
2 tablespoons olive oil
1 green bell pepper, chopped
1 cup chopped onion
3 garlic cloves, chopped
1 (28-ounce) can crushed tomatoes
1 (15-ounce) can chopped tomatoes
1 (15-ounce) can tomato sauce
1/2 cup water

1/4 cup fresh parsley, chopped
1 1/2 teaspoons sugar
1 teaspoon salt, or to taste
1/4 teaspoon garlic powder
1/4 teaspoon pepper
2 or 3 bay leaves
8 ounces thin spaghetti
8 ounces Cheddar cheese, shredded
8 ounces mozzarella cheese, shredded

Brown the ground beef in the olive oil in a saucepan, stirring constantly until crumbly; drain. Stir in the bell pepper, onion and garlic. Cook until the vegetables are tender. Stir in the crushed tomatoes, chopped tomatoes, tomato sauce, water, parsley, sugar, salt, garlic powder, pepper and bay leaves. Bring to a boil and reduce the heat to medium-low. Simmer for 30 minutes. Remove and discard the bay leaves.

Cook the pasta according to the package directions; drain. Mix the Cheddar cheese and mozzarella cheese in a bowl.

Layer one-third of the sauce, one-half of the pasta and one-third of the cheese mixture in a 9×13-inch baking dish sprayed with nonstick cooking spray. Repeat the layers. Top with the remaining sauce. Bake, uncovered, for 45 minutes. Sprinkle with the remaining cheese mixture and bake for 10 to 15 minutes longer. Let stand for 10 minutes. Cut into squares.

Serves 8

*B*lessed is the one who will dine in the Kingdom of God.

Luke 14:15

Vegetables & Side Dishes

THRIFTY STORES

Throughout the country, St. Vincent de Paul Thrift Stores provide a place where the poor can afford to shop. The stores also generate funds for our many charitable outreach programs. The following story, based on the experience of a Thrift Store donor, illustrates how it's possible for someone to visit one of our stores and leave with something of much greater value than the items purchased.

"Now that's more like it….My kitchen cabinets are cleaned out. All the stuff I had, but never used, is packed up and ready to be donated to St. Vincent de Paul. No, it's not spring cleaning time, and I haven't given up cooking. However, I did have an experience the other day that made me stop and reevaluate my priorities.

"I had stopped by a St. Vincent de Paul thrift store to look for a 'fifties' outfit for my daughter for a school party. I found a couple of items that had promise and got in line to check out. While I was standing there, the elderly woman in front of me was searching in the bottom of a rather well-worn purse and was pulling out loose change.

"When it was her turn to check out, she put one plate, a glass, a fork, and mismatched spoon on the counter. The clerk added it up, and as the lady was counting out her change to pay, she said very proudly to the clerk, 'I have two grandchildren living with me, and another granddaughter is coming to stay. I only had three plates, but now I have a plate for her, too!'

"After my initial reaction of pity for this woman, I felt something like embarrassment, almost shame, that I had so much while this woman possessed only the bare minimum. I saw for the first time my personal responsibility to answer Christ's call to share what I have with the least of my brothers and sisters. I also felt humbled at the sight of this woman's joy shining through the shadow of her material poverty."

Store Customer

Speckled Butter Beans with Corn Bread Crust

4 cups chicken broth
2 (16-ounce) packages frozen butter beans
$1/2$ teaspoon salt
$1/2$ teaspoon pepper
1 large sweet onion, chopped
1 poblano chile, chopped
1 tablespoon olive oil
2 cups cornmeal mix
$1/2$ cup buttermilk
$1/2$ cup sour cream
2 eggs, lightly beaten

Combine the broth, beans, salt and pepper in a saucepan. Bring to a boil over medium-high heat. Reduce the heat to low and simmer, covered, for 25 minutes or until the beans are tender; drain.

Sauté the onion and poblano chile in the olive oil in a skillet over medium-high heat for 2 minutes or until tender. Add to the butter beans and mix well. Spoon into a lightly greased 9×13-inch baking dish.

Mix the cornmeal mix, buttermilk, sour cream and eggs in a bowl until smooth. Spread over the bean mixture, sealing to the edge. Bake at 425 degrees for 20 minutes or until the crust is golden brown.

Serves 6 to 8

When they had their fill, He said to His disciples, "Gather the fragments left over, so that nothing will be wasted." So they collected them, and filled twelve wicker baskets with fragments from the five loaves that had been more than they could eat.

John 6:12–13

Not Your Mama's Green Bean Casserole

2 pounds green beans, trimmed and chopped
6 ounces button mushrooms, sliced
1/2 cup sliced red bell pepper
2 tablespoons balsamic vinegar
2 tablespoons olive oil
1/4 to 1/2 teaspoon Italian seasoning,
    Greek seasoning or Creole seasoning
Ground red pepper to taste
1 large onion, sliced
1 tablespoon olive oil
Bread crumbs to taste
6 ounces goat cheese, softened
3 ounces cream cheese, softened
2 tablespoons milk

Combine the beans with a small amount of water in a saucepan. Cook for 5 to 8 minutes or until the beans are tender-crisp. Drain and transfer to a lightly greased 9×9-inch baking dish. Add the mushrooms, bell pepper, balsamic vinegar, 2 tablespoons olive oil, the Italian seasoning and ground red pepper. Toss to mix. Bake at 375 degrees for 15 minutes. Remove from the oven and increase the oven temperature to 400 degrees.

Sauté the onion in 1 tablespoon olive oil in a skillet until tender. Stir in enough bread crumbs to coat the onion. Mix the goat cheese, cream cheese and milk in a bowl until smooth. Spread over the bean mixture. Top with the onion mixture. Bake for 5 to 8 minutes or until heated though. Serve warm.

Serves 8

The bread of deceit is sweet to a man, but afterward his mouth will be filled with gravel.

Proverbs 20:17

Tailgate Party Beans

8 ounces bacon, chopped
1 cup ketchup
1/2 cup packed light brown sugar
1 tablespoon cider vinegar
1 tablespoon Worcestershire sauce
1 tablespoon dry mustard
1 teaspoon pepper
1 pound ground beef
2 onions, finely chopped
2 (15-ounce) cans kidney beans, drained and rinsed
1 (15-ounce) can lima beans, drained and rinsed
1 (15-ounce) can Great Northern beans

Cook the bacon in a small skillet until crisp; drain. Mix the ketchup, brown sugar, vinegar, Worcestershire sauce, dry mustard and pepper in a bowl.

Brown the ground beef with the onions in a large heavy saucepan over medium-high heat, stirring constantly until the ground beef is crumbly; drain. Stir in the kidney beans, lima beans, undrained Great Northern beans, bacon and the ketchup mixture. Pour into a lightly greased 3-quart baking dish. Bake at 300 degrees for 1 hour.

This dish freezes well before baking.

Serves 8 to 10

He who shuts his ear to the cry of the poor will himself also call and not be heard.

Proverbs 21:13

Broccoli with Caper Sauce

1 crown broccoli
1/2 teaspoon salt
1 teaspoon lemon juice
1 cup mayonnaise
1 tablespoon red wine vinegar

1 tablespoon lemon juice
1 tablespoon minced onion
1 tablespoon drained capers, minced
1 teaspoon dill weed
1 hard-cooked egg yolk, crumbled

Combine the broccoli and enough water to come to the depth of 1-inch in a saucepan. Add the salt and 1 teaspoon lemon juice. Bring to a boil and cook for 6 to 8 minutes or until tender-crisp; drain. Chill until serving time. Combine the mayonnaise, vinegar, 1 tablespoon lemon juice, the onion, capers and dill weed in a blender. Process on low for 15 seconds or until blended. Scrape into a bowl and chill, covered, until serving time. To serve, spoon the sauce over the broccoli and sprinkle with the egg yolk. Prepare the broccoli and sauce 4 to 5 hours in advance when possible for the flavor to meld. The sauce is also great served with smoked salmon.

Serves 6

Cabbage Casserole

1 small head cabbage, cut into chunks
1/2 teaspoon salt
6 slices bacon, chopped
1/4 cup (1/2 stick) butter
1/4 cup all-purpose flour

1 teaspoon salt
1/4 teaspoon pepper
2 cups milk
1 cup (4 ounces) shredded
    Cheddar cheese

Combine the cabbage, 1/2 teaspoon salt and enough water to cover in a saucepan. Bring to a boil and cook until the cabbage is tender; drain. Cook the bacon in small skillet until crisp; drain.

Melt the butter in a large skillet over low heat. Stir in the flour, 1 teaspoon salt and the pepper. Remove from the heat. Add the milk gradually, stirring constantly. Return to low heat and cook until smooth and thick. Stir in the cabbage and pour into a 2-quart baking dish. Sprinkle with the bacon and cheese. Bake, uncovered, at 350 degrees for 20 minutes or until bubbly.

Serves 6 to 8

Orange-Glazed Carrots

2 pounds baby carrots
$1/3$ cup sugar
1 tablespoon cornstarch
$1/4$ teaspoon salt
1 cup water

$1/3$ cup frozen orange juice
  concentrate, thawed
3 tablespoons butter
$1/4$ to $1/2$ cup toasted slivered almonds
  (optional)

Fill a saucepan with water to a depth of $1^1/2$ inches. Bring to a boil. Add the carrots and return to a boil. Cook for 10 to 12 minutes or until tender-crisp; drain. Combine the sugar, cornstarch and salt in a saucepan and mix well. Stir in the water, orange juice concentrate and butter. Cook over medium heat until thick and bubbly, stirring constantly. Stir in the carrots and remove to a serving dish. Sprinkle with the almonds.

Serves 6 to 8

Microwave Cauliflower

1 head cauliflower
$1/2$ cup water
$1/2$ cup mayonnaise

$1/4$ cup yellow mustard
8 ounces Cheddar cheese, shredded
Creole seasoning to taste

Trim the leaves and stalk level with the crown of the cauliflower. Place upside down in a 3-quart microwave-safe bowl. Add the water. Microwave on High for 7 minutes; drain. Turn the cauliflower right-side up in the bowl. Mix the mayonnaise and mustard in a bowl until smooth. Spread over the top of the cauliflower. Sprinkle with the cheese and Creole seasoning. Microwave on High for 1 minute longer or until the cheese is melted. Serve warm.

Serves 6

What is the kingdom of God like? To what can I compare it? It is like a mustard seed that a person took and planted in the garden. When it was fully grown, it became a large bush and the birds of the sky dwelt in its branches.

Luke 13:18–19

Cauliflower Gratin

1/4 cup (1/2 stick) butter
1/4 cup all-purpose flour
1/2 teaspoon dry mustard
1/8 teaspoon nutmeg
1 or 2 pinches of cayenne pepper
1 teaspoon salt
1/2 teaspoon black pepper
2 cups warm milk
8 ounces sharp Cheddar cheese, finely shredded
1/2 cup panko (Japanese bread crumbs)
1 head cauliflower florets, or
   2 (16-ounce) packages frozen cauliflower florets, thawed
Salt and black pepper to taste
Paprika to taste

Melt the butter in a saucepan over low heat. Stir in the flour, dry mustard, nutmeg, cayenne pepper, 1 teaspoon salt and 1/2 teaspoon black pepper. Cook over low to medium-low heat for 6 minutes or until smooth and bubbly, stirring constantly. Remove from the heat. Add the milk gradually, stirring constantly. Return to medium heat and bring to a boil. Boil for 1 minute, stirring constantly. Remove from the heat and add 1 1/2 cups of the cheese. Stir until the cheese is melted. Mix the remaining 1/2 cup cheese and the panko in a bowl.

Place the cauliflower in a buttered 9×13-inch baking dish. Season with salt and pepper. Spoon the cheese sauce over the cauliflower and sprinkle with the panko mixture and paprika. Bake at 375 degrees for 20 minutes. Increase the oven temperature to 400 degrees and bake for 10 to 15 minutes longer or until brown and bubbly. Let stand for 5 minutes before serving.

Serves 6 to 8

One kind word can warm up three winter months.

Japanese Proverb

Maque Choux

6 tablespoons butter
3 cups frozen whole kernel corn, thawed
2 1/2 cups frozen Shoe Peg corn, thawed
1 1/4 cups finely chopped onion
1/2 cup finely chopped celery
1/4 cup finely chopped green bell pepper
1/4 cup finely chopped red bell pepper
1 tablespoon minced garlic
1 1/2 tablespoons chopped fresh thyme
Salt to taste
1 tablespoon all-purpose flour
1 (10-ounce) can Rotel chopped tomatoes with green chiles
1/4 cup plus 1 tablespoon heavy cream
Pepper to taste

Melt the butter in a large skillet over medium-high heat. Add the whole kernel corn and Shoe Peg corn and sauté for 5 minutes. Stir in the onion, celery, green bell pepper, red bell pepper, garlic, thyme and salt. Reduce the heat to medium and cook for 15 minutes or until the vegetables are tender, stirring frequently. Stir in the flour and cook for 2 minutes, stirring constantly. Stir in the tomatoes with green chiles and simmer for 10 minutes, stirring occasionally. Reduce the heat to low and stir in the cream. Cook for 10 minutes, stirring occasionally. Season with salt and pepper.

Serves 6 to 8

Maque Choux (pronounced Mock-shoe) is a creamy stewed corn dish. The name comes from the Creole word for corn, maque, *and the French word for cabbage,* choux. *Although cabbage does not appear in the dish today, it is believed to have been in the original casserole.*

Sautéed Mushrooms with Parsley

1/2 small onion, chopped
2 large garlic cloves, cut into halves
1/4 cup olive oil
1 1/2 pounds white mushrooms, sliced thick
1/4 cup dry white wine
1/4 teaspoon salt
1/4 teaspoon freshly ground pepper
2 tablespoons chopped fresh parsley
1 tablespoon grated Parmesan cheese

Sauté the onion and garlic in the olive oil in a skillet over medium-high heat until the garlic is golden brown. Add the mushrooms and sauté for 7 to 10 minutes or until the mushrooms are golden brown and liquid evaporates. Add the wine and reduce the heat to medium-low. Simmer until the liquid evaporates. Season with the salt and pepper. Remove and discard the garlic. Spoon the mushroom mixture into a serving dish. Sprinkle with the parsley and cheese. Serve warm as a side dish or over grilled steak, chicken or fish.

Serves 6

The name of Jesus is the most sweet-tasting nourishment of contemplation, for it feeds and revives those souls that are famished and spiritually hungry.

St. Bernadine of Siena

Curried Okra

1 pound okra
3 tablespoons olive oil
2 onions, cut into quarters and sliced
1/4 teaspoon cayenne pepper, or to taste
1/4 teaspoon mild curry powder, or to taste
1/4 teaspoon turmeric, or to taste
Salt and pepper to taste

Cut the tops and bottoms from the okra pods. Slice into 1/4- to 1/2-inch-thick rounds. Heat the olive oil in a large heavy skillet over medium-high heat to hot but not smoking. Add the okra and cook for 10 minutes or until light brown, turning occasionally. Add the onions, cayenne pepper, curry powder, turmeric, salt and pepper. Cook for 10 minutes or until the onions are tender, stirring frequently. Serve hot.

Serves 6

Thank you to the Louisiana State University Human Ecology Department for donating this wonderful recipe. LSU's Human Ecology Department and the Society of St. Vincent de Paul have worked together to develop a strong relationship. Students from the department volunteer in the dining room and observe firsthand what a hot meal means to those who have nowhere else to turn for this basic necessity.

Smothered Okra and Tomatoes

5 pounds okra
$1/4$ cup canola oil
1 large onion, chopped
1 tablespoon chopped garlic
1 pound Creole tomatoes, peeled and chopped
$1/2$ cup cider vinegar
Ground red pepper to taste
Salt and black pepper to taste

Cut the tops and bottoms from the okra pods. Slice the okra into $1/2$-inch-thick rounds. Heat the canola oil in a large shallow saucepan. Sauté the onion and garlic in the hot oil until tender. Add the okra, tomatoes and vinegar. Reduce the heat to medium-low. Simmer for 1 hour or until tender, stirring frequently and adding water as needed to keep the mixture from sticking to the bottom of the pan. Season with red pepper, salt and black pepper.

This dish may be frozen and added to gumbo recipes.

Serves 16

Okra comes from a large vegetable plant thought to be of African origin. When cut, okra releases a sticky substance with thickening properties. Along with roux, okra is the traditional thickening agent in gumbo.

Black-Eyed Peas with Mushrooms

1 3/4 cups dried black-eyed peas,
    sorted and rinsed
5 cups water
6 tablespoons vegetable oil
1 teaspoon cumin seeds
1 (1-inch) cinnamon stick
1 1/2 onions, chopped
4 garlic cloves, finely chopped
8 ounces mushrooms, sliced
    1/8 inch thick

4 tomatoes, peeled and chopped
2 teaspoons ground coriander
1 teaspoon ground cumin
1/2 teaspoon turmeric
1/4 teaspoon cayenne pepper
3 tablespoons chopped fresh cilantro
    or parsley
1 to 2 teaspoons salt
Freshly ground black pepper to taste

Bring the peas and water to a boil in a 3-quart saucepan. Reduce the heat to low and simmer, covered, for 2 minutes. Turn off the heat and let stand for 1 hour.

Heat the oil in a skillet over medium-high heat. Add the cumin seeds and cinnamon stick. Cook for 5 or 6 seconds and stir in the onions and garlic. Sauté until the onions are brown on the edges. Add the mushrooms and cook until tender, stirring frequently. Stir in the tomatoes, coriander, ground cumin, turmeric and cayenne pepper. Cook for 1 minute, stirring constantly. Reduce the heat to low and simmer, covered, for 10 minutes. Turn off the heat and let stand.

Return the peas to a boil. Reduce the heat to low and simmer, covered, for 20 to 30 minutes or until the peas are tender. Stir in the mushroom mixture, cilantro, salt and black pepper. Simmer, uncovered, over medium-low heat for 30 minutes, stirring occasionally. Remove and discard the cinnamon stick. Serve with hot cooked rice or naan (Indian bread).

Serves 6

This, rather, is the fasting that I wish: releasing those bound unjustly, untying the thongs of the yoke; Setting free the oppressed, breaking every yoke; sharing your bread with the hungry, sheltering the oppressed and the homeless; Clothing the naked when you see them, and not turning your back on your own.

Isaiah 58:6–7

Snap Peas with Roasted Garlic Dressing

4 garlic bulbs
3 tablespoons olive oil
$^1/4$ cup cider vinegar
2 tablespoons Dijon mustard
1 tablespoon olive oil
$^3/4$ teaspoon salt
$^3/4$ teaspoon pepper
2 (16-ounce) packages frozen snap peas
1 red bell pepper, sliced
1 red onion, sliced
$^1/2$ cup (2 ounces) crumbled feta cheese

Remove the outer layers of skin on the garlic bulbs, leaving just the skin on each clove and keeping the bulb intact. Cut $^1/4$ to $^1/2$ inch from the tops of the bulbs, exposing the cloves. Place on a small rimmed baking dish and drizzle 3 tablespoons olive oil over the tops. Bake, covered with foil, at 350 degrees for 55 minutes. Let cool enough to handle and squeeze the garlic cloves out of the skins into a blender. Add the vinegar, Dijon mustard, 1 tablespoon olive oil, the salt and pepper. Process until smooth.

Steam the peas for 5 minutes or until tender; drain. Sauté the bell pepper and onion in a large skilled sprayed with nonstick cooking spray until tender. Stir in the peas, garlic dressing and cheese; toss to mix. Cook until heated through.

Serves 6 to 8

For six years you may sow your land and gather in its produce. But the seventh year, you shall let the land lie untilled and unharvested, that the poor among you may eat of it and the beasts of the field may eat what the poor leave.

Exodus 23:10–11

Garlic Mashed Potatoes

5 garlic cloves, minced
1 tablespoon olive oil
8 cups water
2 cups low-sodium chicken broth
3 1/2 pounds Yukon gold potatoes,
   peeled and chopped

1/4 teaspoon salt
1 1/2 cups warm buttermilk
1/2 cup (1 stick) butter, melted
1 teaspoon salt
3/4 teaspoon pepper
1/4 cup chopped fresh chives

Sauté the garlic in the olive oil in a 5-quart saucepan over medium heat for 3 minutes. Add the water, broth, potatoes and 1/4 teaspoon salt. Bring to a boil. Reduce the heat and simmer, covered, for 15 to 20 minutes or until the potatoes are tender; drain. Add the buttermilk, butter, 1 teaspoon salt and the pepper. Mash with a large fork or potato masher. Stir in the chives and serve immediately.

Serves 6

Make all you can, save all you can, give all you can.

John Wesley, Christian Theologian

Rosemary and Goat Cheese Smashed Potatoes

2 pounds small red potatoes,
   cut into quarters
1/2 cup (1 stick) butter
8 ounces goat cheese, softened
4 garlic cloves, minced

1/4 to 1/2 cup cream
4 teaspoons chopped fresh rosemary
1/4 teaspoon salt
1/4 teaspoon freshly ground pepper

Combine the potatoes with enough water to cover in a large saucepan. Bring to a boil. Reduce the heat and simmer, covered, for 8 to 10 minutes or until the potatoes are tender; drain. Remove the potatoes to a bowl. Add the butter, cheese, garlic, 1/4 cup of the cream, the rosemary, salt and pepper. Mash with a potato masher, adding the remaining cream until of the desired consistency. Serve immediately.

Serves 8 to 10

Spicy Potato and Corn Casserole

4 ears of corn, or 2^1/2 cups frozen corn kernels, thawed
1 to 2 (10-ounce) cans Rotel chopped tomatoes with green chiles
2^1/2 pounds Yukon gold potatoes, peeled and sliced
Salt and pepper to taste
3 to 4 tablespoons butter
2 cups buttermilk
2 tablespoons chopped chives
2 cups (8 ounces) shredded Monterey Jack cheese

Cut the kernels from the ears of corn with a sharp knife. Drain the tomatoes with green chiles, reserving 1/4 cup of the liquid. Layer one-half of the potatoes in a buttered 9×13-inch baking dish. Season with salt and pepper. Layer one-half of the corn and one-half of the drained tomatoes with green chiles. Dot with the butter. Repeat the layers. Mix the buttermilk and reserved 1/4 cup tomato liquid in a small bowl. Pour over the vegetables.

Bake at 375 degrees for 1 hour or until the potatoes are tender. Sprinkle with the chives and cheese. Bake until the cheese is melted. Let stand for 5 minutes before serving.

Serves 8

All you who are thirsty, come to the water! You who have no money, come, receive grain and eat; Come, without paying and without cost, drink wine and milk! Why spend your money for what is not bread; your wages for what fails to satisfy? Heed me, and you shall eat well, you shall delight in rich fare.

Isaiah 55:1–2

Potatoes Supreme

2 pounds white potatoes (about 6)
Salt to taste
2 cups sour cream
2 cups (8 ounces) shredded
   Cheddar cheese

$1/2$ cup (1 stick) butter, melted
$1/2$ cup chopped green onions
1 (4-ounce) can chopped green chiles
Pepper to taste

Combine the potatoes and a small amount of salted water in a saucepan. Cook until tender; drain. Chill, covered, for 8 to 10 hours. Grate the potatoes into a bowl. Stir in the sour cream, cheese, butter, green onions and green chiles. Season with salt and pepper. Spoon into an $1 1/2$-quart baking dish sprayed with nonstick cooking spray. Bake, covered, at 350 degrees for 35 minutes.

Serves 6 to 8

Potato and Artichoke Casserole

2 pounds red potatoes, peeled
1 cup chopped onion
5 to 6 garlic cloves, chopped
$3/4$ cup extra-virgin olive oil

2 (14-ounce) cans artichoke hearts,
   drained and quartered
1 cup Italian bread crumbs
1 cup (4 ounces) grated
   Parmesan cheese

Combine the potatoes and enough water to cover in a saucepan. Bring to a boil and cook until tender; drain. Slice the potatoes.

Sauté the onion and garlic in the olive oil in a skillet over medium heat for 10 to 15 minutes. Combine the potatoes, artichoke hearts, bread crumbs and cheese. Toss to mix. Add the onion mixture and toss to mix. Remove to an 8×8-inch baking dish. Bake at 350 degrees for 15 minutes or until heated through. This recipe may be doubled and baked in a 9×13-inch baking dish.

Serves 8

The war against hunger is truly mankind's war of liberation.

John F. Kennedy, 35th President of the United States

Parmesan Scalloped Potatoes

1/2 onion, sliced
1/3 cup butter
2 pounds Yukon gold potatoes, peeled and thinly sliced
3 cups whipping cream
1/4 cup flat-leaf parsley, chopped
2 garlic cloves, chopped
1 1/2 teaspoons salt
1/4 teaspoon freshly ground black pepper
1/4 teaspoon cayenne pepper
1/2 cup (2 ounces) grated Parmesan cheese

Sauté the onion in the butter in a large heavy saucepan over medium-high heat for 3 minutes. Stir in the potatoes, cream, parsley, garlic, salt, black pepper and cayenne pepper. Bring to a boil and reduce the heat to medium-low. Simmer for 15 minutes or until the potatoes are tender. Spoon into a lightly greased 9×13-inch baking dish. Sprinkle with the cheese. Bake at 400 degrees for 25 to 30 minutes or until bubbly and golden brown. Cool on a wire rack for 10 minutes before serving.

Serves 6 to 8

Don't dig your grave with your own knife and fork.

English Proverb

Sweet Potato Fries with Mango Chutney Mayonnaise

3 (14-ounce) large sweet potatoes
3 small eggs
3 tablespoons water
1 cup seasoned bread crumbs
6 tablespoons grated Parmesan cheese
3/4 teaspoon black pepper
3/4 teaspoon red pepper
3/4 cup mayonnaise
6 tablespoons mango chutney
3/4 teaspoon curry powder

Peel and slice the sweet potatoes into 1/4-inch-thick strips. Whisk the eggs and water in a shallow bowl until combined. Combine the bread crumbs, cheese, black pepper and red pepper in a sealable plastic bag and mix well.

Dip the sweet potato strips in batches into the egg wash and add immediately to the bread crumb mixture. Seal the bag and shake to coat.

Arrange in a single layer on a baking sheet sprayed with olive oil nonstick cooking spray. Spray the sweet potatoes with the olive oil cooking spray. Bake at 450 degrees for 25 to 30 minutes or until golden brown and crisp.

Mix the mayonnaise, chutney and curry powder in a bowl until smooth.
Serve with the sweet potato fries.

Serves 6 to 8

A smiling face is half the meal.

Latvian Proverb

Grilled Sweet Potatoes

4 sweet potatoes, sliced into
   1/4-inch-thick rounds
2 tablespoons olive oil

Garlic salt to taste
Italian seasoning to taste

Arrange the sweet potatoes on a large sheet of heavy-duty foil. Drizzle with the olive oil and sprinkle with garlic salt and Italian seasoning. Toss to mix. Cover with another sheet of heavy-duty foil and fold the edges together, sealing tightly. Place on a grill rack over indirect heat and grill for 20 to 25 minutes or until the sweet potatoes are tender. Remove to a platter and poke three or four holes in the bag to let the steam escape before opening the packet.

Serves 4

Stuffed Sweet Potatoes

3 pounds small to medium
   sweet potatoes
2 tablespoons butter
1/3 cup cream
1/2 cup packed light brown sugar
1/3 cup dried cranberries
1 teaspoon vanilla extract

1/2 teaspoon cinnamon
1/4 cup all-purpose flour
1/3 cup chopped pecans
1/4 cup packed brown sugar
2 tablespoons butter, melted
1 teaspoon vanilla extract
1/4 teaspoon cinnamon

Place the sweet potatoes on a baking sheet. Bake at 400 degrees for 1 hour or until tender. Slice a small portion off of the top side of the sweet potatoes. Scoop the pulp into a bowl, leaving a 1/4-inch shell. Mash the pulp. Stir in 2 tablespoons butter, the cream, 1/2 cup brown sugar, the cranberries, 1 teaspoon vanilla and 1/2 teaspoon cinnamon. Spoon the pulp mixture into the sweet potato shells.

Mix the flour, pecans, 1/4 cup brown sugar, 2 tablespoons butter, 1 teaspoon vanilla and 1/4 teaspoon cinnamon in a bowl. Sprinkle over the sweet potatoes. Bake at 350 degrees for 15 to 20 minutes or until the tops are brown and the potatoes are heated through.

Serves 4 to 6

Sweet Potato Casserole

4 pounds sweet potatoes, peeled and cut into quarters
1³/4 cups packed light brown sugar
³/4 cup (1¹/2 sticks) butter, chopped
¹/2 cup milk or half-and-half
4 eggs, beaten
3 to 4 tablespoons lemon juice
2 tablespoons grated orange zest (optional)
1 cup chopped prosciutto (optional)
1 tablespoon chopped fresh rosemary (optional)

Combine the sweet potatoes with enough water to cover in a large heavy saucepan. Bring to a boil. Reduce the heat to medium-low and simmer, covered, for 15 to 20 minutes or until tender; drain. Mash with a potato masher in the saucepan. Stir in the brown sugar, butter, milk, eggs and lemon juice. Stir in orange zest. Spoon into a lightly greased 3-quart rectangular baking dish. Top with the prosciutto and rosemary. Bake, uncovered, at 350 degrees for 30 to 35 minutes. Let stand for 10 minutes before serving.

For a variation, substitute ¹/2 cup peanut butter for the orange zest and 1 cup chopped peanuts and ¹/2 cup shredded coconut for the topping; or 2 to 4 teaspoons red curry paste for the orange zest and 1 sliced large onion and 2 thinly sliced garlic cloves, sautéed, for the topping; or 2 tablespoons bourbon for the orange zest and 1 cup brown sugar, ²/3 cup all-purpose flour, ²/3 cup melted butter and 1 cup chopped pecans for the topping; or one drained 8-ounce can pineapple for the orange zest and miniature marshmallows added at the last 10 minutes of baking for the topping.

Serves 8 to 10

Sweet potatoes grown in Louisiana are commonly referred to as "yams." They are soft, high in natural sugar, moist, and have a bright orange flesh. True yams come from tropical and subtropical regions of the world.

Spinach and Monterey Jack Bread Pudding

1 (16-ounce) loaf French
   bread, cut into cubes
1 cup chopped onion
1 tablespoon minced garlic
1/4 cup (1/2 stick) butter
8 ounces mushrooms, sliced
5 eggs
1 1/2 cups milk
1 (12-ounce) can evaporated milk

1/2 teaspoon Creole seasoning
1/4 teaspoon salt
1/4 teaspoon black pepper
1/4 teaspoon red pepper
1 (10-ounce) package frozen spinach,
   thawed and drained
2 cups (8 ounces) Monterey
   Jack cheese
1/3 cup shredded Parmesan cheese

Arrange the bread on a baking sheet. Bake at 300 degrees for 10 minutes or until golden brown and dry. Cool on the baking sheet on a wire rack. Increase the oven temperature to 375 degrees.

Sauté the onion and garlic in the butter in a skillet over medium heat for 3 minutes. Stir in the mushrooms and reduce the heat to medium-low. Cook, covered, for 8 minutes or until the mushrooms are tender. Remove from the heat and cool slightly.

Whisk the eggs in a large bowl until frothy. Whisk in the milk, evaporated milk, Creole seasoning, salt, black pepper and red pepper. Stir in the mushroom mixture, spinach, Monterey Jack cheese and bread. Let stand for 10 minutes or until most of the liquid is absorbed. Pour into a 9×13-inch baking dish. Bake at 300 degrees for 35 minutes. Sprinkle with the Parmesan cheese. Bake for 10 minutes longer or until the center is firm, puffed and brown. Let stand for 10 minutes before serving.

Serves 6

The pillar of the world is hope.

African Proverb

Party Spinach

4 (10-ounce) packages frozen chopped spinach
1/4 cup (1/2 stick) butter
8 ounces cream cheese, chopped and softened
Juice of 1 lemon
Salt and pepper to taste
8 ounces mushrooms, sliced
1 (8-ounce) can sliced water chestnuts, drained
1 (14-ounce) can artichoke hearts, drained and
    cut into quarters
Seasoned bread crumbs

Cook the spinach according to the package directions. Drain, squeezing out any excess moisture. Melt the butter in a large saucepan over medium heat. Add the cream cheese and cook until melted, stirring constantly. Stir in the spinach and lemon juice. Season with salt and pepper.

Layer the mushrooms, water chestnuts and artichoke hearts in a 3-quart baking dish sprayed with nonstick cooking spray. Spread the spinach mixture over the artichoke hearts. Sprinkle with bread crumbs. Bake at 350 degrees for 25 to 30 minutes or until heated through.

Serves 12

Let food be your medicine and medicine be your food.

Hippocrates

Squash Casserole

8 yellow squash
Salt and black pepper to taste
1 onion, chopped
1/2 cup (1 stick) butter
2 eggs, lightly beaten
1 cup (4 ounces) shredded sharp Cheddar cheese
3/4 cup mayonnaise
1/2 cup butter cracker crumbs
1/4 teaspoon ground red pepper

Slice the squash into 1/4-inch-thick rounds. Bring enough water to cover the squash to a boil in a saucepan. Add the squash and season with salt and pepper. Cook until tender; drain. Sauté the onion in the butter in a skillet until tender. Remove from the heat and cool slightly.

Combine the eggs, cheese, mayonnaise, cracker crumbs and red pepper in a bowl and mix well. Fold in the squash and onion. Season with salt and pepper. Spoon into a greased 9×13-inch baking dish. Bake at 350 degrees for 30 minutes.

Serves 8 to 10

Cookery is not chemistry. It is an art.

Marcel Boulestin, Famous French Chef

Mirlitons with Shrimp

4 large mirlitons (chayotes)
12 ounces peeled shrimp
1 large onion, chopped
2 ribs celery, chopped
2 green onions, chopped
2 garlic cloves, chopped

6 tablespoons butter
3/4 cup Italian bread crumbs
1 tablespoon Creole seasoning
1 teaspoon dried parsley
1/4 cup Italian bread crumbs
1 teaspoon salt

Slice the mirlitons into halves. Remove and discard the pits. Bring enough water to cover the mirlitons to a boil in a saucepan. Add the mirlitons and reduce the heat to medium. Cook until tender. Drain, reserving some of the liquid. Peel and mash the mirlitons in a bowl.

Sauté the shrimp, onion, celery, green onions and garlic in the butter in a skillet over medium heat for 10 minutes or until the vegetables are tender. Add some of the reserved liquid if the vegetables begin to stick to the skillet. Stir in the mirlitons and 3/4 cup bread crumbs, the Creole seasoning and parsley. Spoon into a lightly greased 2-quart baking dish. Sprinkle with 1/4 cup bread crumbs. Bake, uncovered, at 350 degrees for 20 to 30 minutes or until heated through.

Serves 6

Barukh ata Adonai Eloheinu Melekh ha olam, bo're p'ri ha gafen.
Blessed are You, Lord our God, King of the universe, who creates the fruit of the vine.

Jewish Blessing Prayer

Italian Vegetables

1 cup chopped onion
3 garlic cloves, minced
3 tablespoons olive oil
1 pound eggplant, unpeeled and
   coarsely chopped
2 cups chopped zucchini
2 cups chopped yellow squash
1 cup chopped yellow or orange
   bell pepper
2 cups sliced mushrooms

1 (15-ounce) can Italian-style
   tomatoes, drained and chopped, or
   1 (15-ounce) can chopped
   tomatoes, 2 teaspoons dried basil
   and 1 teaspoon dried oregano
2 tablespoons tomato paste
Salt and pepper to taste
1/2 cup (2 ounces) grated
   Parmesan cheese

Sauté the onion and garlic in the olive oil in skillet over medium heat for 5 minutes or until tender. Add the eggplant and sauté for 5 minutes. Add the zucchini, yellow squash, bell pepper and mushrooms and sauté for 5 minutes. Stir in the tomatoes and tomato paste. Bring to a boil. Reduce the heat to low and simmer, covered, for 15 minutes or until the vegetables are tender, stirring occasionally. Season with salt and pepper. Spoon into a 9×9-inch baking dish. Sprinkle with the cheese.

Chill, covered, for several hours to allow the flavors to meld. Let stand at room temperature for 15 minutes. Bake, covered, at 350 degrees for 30 minutes or until heated through. Let stand for 5 minutes before serving.

Serves 8

We thank You Lord, Giver of all good things, for these Your gifts and all Your mercies, and we bless Your holy name forever. Amen.

Eastern Orthodox Prayer

Vegetable Casserole

1 cup half-and-half
1 cup mayonnaise
$1/2$ cup (2 ounces) grated Parmesan cheese
$1/2$ cup (2 ounces) shredded Cheddar cheese
$1/2$ cup chopped onion
$1/2$ cup chopped green bell pepper
$1/4$ cup ($1/2$ stick) butter
16 ounces frozen French-style green beans,
    thawed and drained
1 (14- to 16-ounce) package baby lima beans,
    thawed and drained
16 ounces frozen green peas, thawed and drained

Mix the half-and-half, mayonnaise, Parmesan cheese and Cheddar cheese in a bowl. Sauté the onion and bell pepper in the butter in a skillet over medium heat until tender. Let cool slightly and stir into the mayonnaise mixture.

Combine the green beans, lima beans and peas in a shallow 2-quart baking dish sprayed with nonstick cooking spray. Toss to mix. Spread the mayonnaise mixture over the beans and peas. Bake at 325 degrees for 50 minutes.

Serves 8

If a brother or sister has nothing to wear and has no food for the day, and one of you says to them, "Go in peace, keep warm, and eat well," but you do not give them the necessities of the body, what good is it?

James 2:15–16

Tahini Roasted Vegetables

1 eggplant, peeled and cut into
   1-inch pieces
2 red bell peppers, cut into
   1-inch pieces
1 onion, cut into 1-inch pieces
1 zucchini, cut into 1-inch pieces
2 small yellow squash, cut into
   1-inch pieces

1 tablespoon olive oil
1 tablespoon tahini
2 teaspoons rice wine vinegar
2 teaspoons honey
1/2 teaspoon salt
1/4 teaspoon pepper
2 tablespoons minced fresh parsley

Mix the eggplant, bell peppers, onion, zucchini and yellow squash on a 10×15-inch rimmed baking sheet sprayed with nonstick cooking spray. Whisk the olive oil, tahini, vinegar, honey, salt and pepper in a bowl until combined. Drizzle over the vegetables. Toss to mix. Bake at 450 degrees for 25 to 30 minutes or until tender, stirring occasionally. Add the parsley and toss to mix.

Serves 6

Some seed fell on rich soil and produced fruit. It came up and grew and yielded thirty, sixty, and a hundredfold.

Mark 4:8

Scalloped Pineapple

1 cup (2 sticks) butter, melted
3 eggs, beaten
1 (20-ounce) can crushed
   pineapple, drained

8 slices white bread, crusts trimmed
   and bread chopped
1 3/4 cups sugar

Mix the butter and eggs in a bowl. Add the pineapple and bread and toss to mix. Add the sugar and toss to mix. Pour into a greased 8×12-inch baking dish. Bake at 325 degrees for 45 minutes. Serve warm or cold.

Serves 8 to 10

Mushroom Couscous

3 to 4 tablespoons extra-virgin olive oil
4 cups sliced mushrooms
$1/2$ cup chopped onion
3 garlic cloves, minced
1 cup low-sodium beef broth
1 teaspoon minced fresh thyme
$1/4$ to $1/2$ teaspoon Tabasco sauce
$1/4$ teaspoon salt
$1/4$ teaspoon freshly ground pepper
$2/3$ cup uncooked couscous

Heat the olive oil in a 4-quart saucepan over medium heat. Add the mushrooms, onion and garlic and cook for 5 to 7 minutes or until tender, stirring constantly. Stir in the broth, thyme, hot sauce, salt and pepper. Bring to a boil and stir in the couscous. Remove from the heat and cover. Let stand for 5 minutes. Fluff with a fork.

Serves 4

Happy are you who are hungry now; you shall be satisfied.

Luke 6:21

Tabbouli

2 cups boiling water
1 cup bulger wheat
2 tomatoes, finely chopped
1 bunch green onions, sliced
2 cups finely chopped parsley

3 teaspoons chopped fresh mint
1/2 cup fresh lemon juice
1/4 cup olive oil
Salt and freshly ground pepper
  to taste

Pour the boiling water over the bulger wheat in a bowl. Let stand for 1 hour, stirring occasionally. Drain through a fine wire strainer and return the bulger wheat to the bowl. Fold in tomatoes, green onions, parsley, mint, lemon juice and olive oil. Season with salt and pepper. Chill, covered, for 2 hours. Serve with roasted lamb and stuffed grape leaves or as an appetizer with toasted pita chips.

Serves 8

Curried Rice

4 cups sliced mushrooms
2 garlic cloves, minced
3 tablespoons extra-virgin olive oil
1 teaspoon curry powder
1/2 teaspoon cumin seeds, ground
2 cups reduced-sodium vegetable
  broth or chicken broth

1 cup frozen cut green beans, thawed
1 cup long grain rice
8 slices Canadian bacon, cut into
  short thin strips
1/2 teaspoon pepper

Sauté the mushrooms and garlic in the olive oil in a 3-quart saucepan over medium heat for 5 minutes. Stir in the curry powder and cumin seeds. Cook for 30 seconds. Stir in the broth and bring to a boil. Stir in the green beans and rice. Reduce the heat to low and simmer, covered, for 18 to 20 minutes or until the rice is tender and the liquid is absorbed. Stir in the bacon and pepper. Cook until the bacon is heated through. Serve warm.

Serves 8

Dirty Rice

1 onion, chopped
1 large bell pepper, chopped
5 or 6 garlic cloves, chopped
2 or 3 cayenne chiles, or 1 serrano chile and
   1 hot red chile, chopped
1 teaspoon dried parsley
1 teaspoon salt
1 pound ground beef
1 pound bulk pork sausage
2 (4- to 6-ounce) cans of mushroom steak sauce
3 to 4 cups cooked rice

Combine the onion, bell pepper, garlic, chiles, parsley and salt in a blender. Process until almost smooth. Brown the ground beef and sausage in a skillet over medium heat, stirring constantly until crumbly; drain. Stir in the onion mixture. Simmer for 10 minutes. Stir in the steak sauce and reduce the heat to medium-low. Simmer, covered, for 30 minutes, stirring occasionally. Add the rice gradually, stirring constantly until the mixture has equal portions of meat and rice. Cook until heated through.

Serves 8 to 10

The Conrad Rice Mill, located in New Iberia, Louisiana, is the oldest working rice mill in America. In the 1950s "KONRIKO" was trademarked as an acronym for "CONRAD RICE COMPANY." The mill was placed on the National Register of Historic Places in 1981.

Crawfish Rice

4 cups low-sodium vegetable broth or chicken broth
2 1/2 cups long grain rice
1 cup chopped red onion
3 garlic cloves, minced
1 1/2 teaspoons salt
1 1/4 teaspoons chili powder
1/2 teaspoon turmeric
1/4 teaspoon black pepper
1 bay leaf
1 to 2 tablespoons olive oil
1 red bell pepper, julienned
1 orange bell pepper, julienned

4 green onions, chopped
4 garlic cloves, minced
2 teaspoons chopped fresh parsley
1/2 teaspoon dried basil
1/2 teaspoon dried thyme
1/4 to 1/2 teaspoon Tabasco sauce
1 1/2 cups sliced mushrooms
1 pound crawfish tails
1/4 teaspoon ground red pepper, or to taste
1 cup grape tomatoes
1 cup frozen green peas
1/2 cup pecans, chopped and toasted

Combine the broth, rice, onion, 3 garlic cloves, the salt, chili powder, turmeric, black pepper and bay leaf in saucepan. Bring to a boil. Reduce the heat to medium-low and simmer, covered, for 20 minutes or until the rice is tender. Remove and discard the bay leaf.

Heat the olive oil in a large skillet over medium-high heat. Add the red bell pepper, orange bell pepper, green onions, 4 garlic cloves, the parsley, basil, thyme and hot sauce. Cook for 2 minutes, stirring constantly. Stir in the mushrooms and cook until the bell peppers are tender-crisp, stirring constantly. Add the crawfish and ground red pepper. Cook for 3 minutes, stirring frequently. Stir in the tomatoes and peas. Cook until heated through, stirring frequently. Remove from the heat and stir in the rice. Spoon into a serving dish. Sprinkle with the pecans.

Serves 15 to 20

Talk doesn't cook rice.

Chinese Proverb

Wild Rice Pilaf

4 cups vegetable broth or low-sodium chicken broth
3 large shallots, minced
2 tablespoons unsalted butter
1 tablespoon canola oil
2 cups wild rice
1/2 cup dried cranberries
1 bay leaf
2 fresh thyme sprigs
1/2 teaspoon fine sea salt
1/8 teaspoon white pepper
1/2 cup toasted pecans, coarsely chopped
1/4 cup minced fresh flat-leaf parsley

Bring the broth to a simmer in a 3-quart saucepan over medium heat. Sauté the shallots in the butter and canola oil in a skillet over medium heat for 4 to 5 minutes or until translucent. Stir in the rice and cook for 3 minutes, stirring constantly. Stir the rice mixture into the broth. Add the cranberries, bay leaf, thyme, 1/2 teaspoon salt and 1/8 teaspoon pepper. Bring to a simmer, stirring occasionally.

Pour into a 2-quart baking dish sprayed with nonstick cooking spray. Bake, covered, at 375 degrees for 40 to 45 minutes or until the liquid is absorbed and the rice is tender. Remove and discard the bay leaf and thyme sprigs. Season with additional salt and pepper. Stir in the pecans and parsley. Serve hot or warm.

Serves 8 to 10

Baked Orzo with Fontina Cheese and Peas

4 cups low-sodium chicken broth
16 ounces orzo
1 cup chopped onion
3 tablespoons butter
8 ounces mushrooms, sliced
1 cup marsala
1/2 cup heavy cream
4 ounces fontina cheese, shredded
4 ounces fresh mozzarella cheese, chopped
1 cup frozen green peas, thawed
1/2 teaspoon salt
1/2 teaspoon freshly ground pepper
1/2 cup bread crumbs
1/4 cup (1 ounce) grated Parmesan cheese
1 teaspoon dried thyme

Bring the broth to a boil in a saucepan over medium-high heat. Stir in the pasta and cook for 7 minutes or until almost tender. Pour into a large bowl.

Sauté the onion in the butter in a skillet over medium heat for 3 minutes or until tender. Add the mushrooms and cook for 7 minutes or until the edges turn golden brown, stirring frequently. Add the wine gradually, stirring constantly and scraping up any brown bits from the bottom of the skillet. Cook for 5 minutes or until the wine is reduced by half. Stir into the pasta mixture. Stir in the cream, fontina cheese, mozzarella cheese, peas, salt and pepper. Pour into a 9×13-inch baking dish sprayed with nonstick cooking spray. Mix the bread crumbs, Parmesan cheese and thyme in a bowl. Sprinkle over the pasta mixture. Bake at 400 degrees for 25 minutes. Serve warm

Serves 6 to 8

Like merchant ships, she secures her provisions from afar. She rises while it is still night, and distributes food to her household.

Proverbs 31:14–15

Desserts

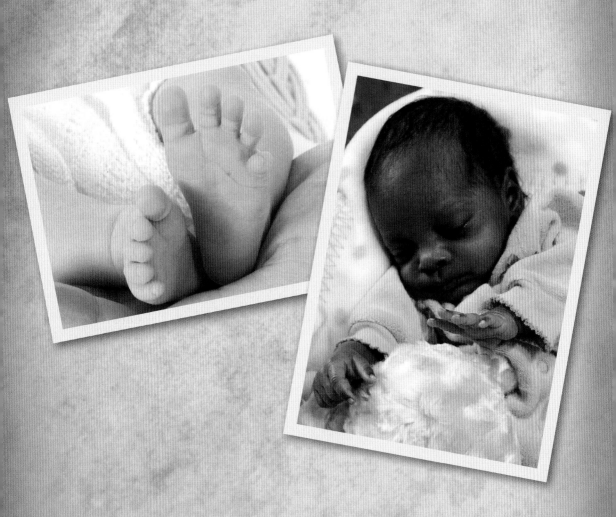

Sweet Dreams

The Society of St. Vincent de Paul provides safe housing and assistance to many people in crisis. With a philosophy of helping people to break the cycle of homelessness, the Bishop Ott Shelter for men and Sweet Dreams Shelter for women and children provide a hand-up of hope to those who have nowhere else to turn. One of the beautiful fruits of this ministry—its effect on the volunteers that serve this vulnerable population—is captured in the following story.

"My whole perspective on giving changed last Christmas. I was standing in front of a discount store, helping a group of volunteers collect items for the Sweet Dreams Shelter. It was a rainy day, just before Christmas, and the store was a madhouse, with hundreds of harried shoppers passing in and out during the few hours I was there. As shoppers hurried by, we handed out lists of items our shelter needed.

"The weather was bitterly cold, and it had begun to rain a little harder. Not everyone who went past took one of our lists, but most people came back out with an item or two for our collection, and others donated shopping carts full of everything from dolls to detergent.

"Toward the end of the drive, a young woman approached us with a bag of groceries to donate. She had her hands full, with one child in a stroller and another tugging on her arm. She handed over her items with a big smile and a hug for one of our shelter staff members helping out with the collection. When he asked how she was doing, she said, 'I'm doing great. I've got a good job now, and we have an apartment nearby.'

'She really seemed to have the Christmas spirit of giving,' I said after she'd gone. 'How do you know her?'

'This time last year,' he said, 'she was living at our shelter.'

"I couldn't help but think of the Bible story of the widow's mite. Neither the widow nor the young mother had much to give, but they, recipients of God's love, responded willingly and joyfully to Christ's call to be Christ to others. Sometimes that requires we give from our necessity rather than from our abundance."

Sweet Dreams Shelter Volunteer

Beignets

1 cup milk
2 tablespoons shortening
2 tablespoons granulated sugar
1 envelope dry yeast
1 egg, lightly beaten
3 cups all-purpose flour
1 teaspoon salt
Vegetable oil for frying
Confectioners' sugar for dusting

Combine the milk, shortening and granulated sugar in a small saucepan. Cook over low heat until smooth, stirring frequently. Pour into a large mixing bowl and let stand to cool to 105 to 115 degrees. Dissolve the yeast in the milk mixture. Let stand for 5 minutes. Stir in the egg. Combine the flour and salt. Add $1^1/2$ cups of the flour mixture to the yeast mixture. Beat at medium speed for 1 minute or until smooth. Add enough of the remaining flour mixture gradually to a make a soft dough. Place in a greased bowl, turning to coat the surface. Let rise, covered, in a warm place away from drafts until doubled in bulk.

Punch the dough down. Knead on a floured surface four or five times. Roll into a 12×15-inch rectangle. Cut into 3-inch strips. Cut each strip into four diagonal strips. Let rise, covered, on a floured surface in a warm place away from drafts for 30 minutes or until doubled in bulk. Slide, in batches, into 360-degree oil 3 inches deep in a Dutch oven. Fry for 3 to 5 minutes or until golden brown, turning once. Drain on a wire rack. Cool slightly. Dust with confectioners' sugar. Serve immediately.

Makes 20

Beignets, a New Orleans specialty, are sweet like doughnuts but are square shaped and without a hole. The word "beignet" (pronounced ben-YAY) comes from the early Celtic word "bigne" meaning "to raise." It is also French for "fritter."

Sfinges

2 eggs
2 cups all-purpose flour
$3/4$ cup (about) milk
$1/2$ cup granulated sugar
3 teaspoons (heaping) baking powder
1 teaspoon vanilla extract
Vegetable oil for frying
Confectioners' sugar for dusting (optional)
$1/2$ cup granulated sugar (optional)
$1/2$ teaspoon cinnamon (optional)

Beat the eggs in a large mixing bowl until foamy. Add the flour, $3/4$ cup milk, $1/2$ cup sugar, the baking powder and vanilla. Beat until combined. The dough will be thick. Add additional milk if needed to form a dough. Let stand for 5 minutes.

Drop by tablespoonfuls in batches into deep 375-degree oil in a deep skillet or deep fryer. Fry until the dough floats to the top and both sides are golden brown, turning as needed. Remove with a slotted spoon and drain on paper towels. Roll in confectioners' sugar or shake in a small nonrecyclable paper bag with a mixture of $1/2$ cup granulated sugar and $1/2$ teaspoon cinnamon.

Serves 6

Just about every culture has some sort of fried dough in their arsenal. For the Italians, it is sfinges, also referred to as zeppole. Whatever you want to call them, Italian fried dough dipped in sugar is a great treat for yourself and the kids.

Sweet Potato Bread Pudding

Bread Pudding

1 (16-ounce) loaf day-old French
    bread, cut into bite-size pieces

1 1/2 cups mashed cooked sweet
    potatoes, or 1 (29-ounce) can
    sweet potatoes, drained
    and mashed

1 (12-ounce) can evaporated milk

2 1/4 cups half-and-half

4 eggs, lightly beaten

3 tablespoons cane syrup

1 cup packed light brown sugar

1 1/2 teaspoons cinnamon

1/2 teaspoon nutmeg

2 teaspoons vanilla extract

Praline Sauce

1 1/4 cups packed light brown sugar

3/4 cup heavy cream

1 tablespoon butter

1/2 teaspoon vanilla extract

1/2 cup chopped pecans, toasted

To prepare the bread pudding, arrange the bread in a single layer on a baking sheet. Bake at 300 degrees for 10 minutes or until dry and light golden brown. Remove from the oven and let stand to cool. Increase the oven temperature to 350 degrees.

Combine the sweet potatoes, evaporated milk, half-and-half, eggs, cane syrup, brown sugar, cinnamon, nutmeg and vanilla in a mixing bowl. Beat on low speed for 30 seconds. Beat on medium speed for 1 minute or until blended. Stir in the bread, coating with the sweet potato mixture. Spoon into a 9×13-inch baking dish sprayed with nonstick cooking spray. Let stand for 15 minutes. Bake for 30 to 40 minutes or until the center is firm.

To prepare the sauce, combine the brown sugar, cream and butter in a saucepan. Cook over medium-high heat until the butter is melted, stirring frequently. Bring to a gentle boil. Boil for 2 minutes, stirring constantly. Remove from the heat and stir in the vanilla and pecans. Let stand for 5 minutes, stirring occasionally.

To serve, spoon the warm bread pudding onto dessert dishes. Spoon the warm sauce over the top.

Serves 15

The many plantation homes along the Mississippi River were built when sugar cane fields earned Louisiana the title of the "Sugar Bowl" of the country.

Piña Colada Bread Pudding

Bread Pudding

3 eggs, beaten
1 1/2 cups sugar
1/4 cup (1/2 stick) butter
1 (13-ounce) can coconut milk
1 (5-ounce) can evaporated milk
5 ounces water
1 tablespoon vanilla extract
1 teaspoon coconut extract
1/2 teaspoon salt
8 ounces pineapple chunks, drained
   and cut into halves

1/2 cup sweetened flaked coconut
1 (6-ounce) loaf day-old French bread

Rum Sauce

1 tablespoon cornstarch
2/3 cup heavy cream
2/3 cup sugar
1/4 cup rum
2 tablespoons butter
1 teaspoon vanilla extract

To prepare the bread pudding, mix the eggs, sugar, butter, coconut milk, evaporated milk, water, vanilla, coconut extract and salt in a large bowl until smooth. Stir in the pineapple and coconut. Tear the bread into bite-size pieces and stir into the milk mixture. Let stand for 1 hour or until the bread has absorbed all of the liquid. Pour into a 9×13-inch baking pan. Place the baking dish in a larger baking dish. Add hot water to the larger dish to a depth of 1/2 to 3/4 inch. Bake at 325 degrees for 1 hour. Let stand to cool slightly before serving.

To prepare the rum sauce, dissolve the cornstarch in the cream in a saucepan. Add the sugar, rum, butter and vanilla. Bring to a boil over medium-high heat, stirring frequently. Remove from the heat.

To serve, spoon the warm bread pudding onto dessert dishes. Spoon the warm sauce over the top.

Serves 12 to 15

The bread of charity is life itself for the needy.

Sirach 34:21a

Chocolate Mousse Trifle

Chocolate Mousse
1 envelope unflavored gelatin
2 tablespoons cold water
1/4 cup boiling water
1 cup sugar
1/2 cup baking cocoa
2 cups cold heavy whipping cream
2 teaspoons vanilla extract

Assembly
1 (21-ounce) package brownie mix,
　prepared
1/2 cup chocolate syrup
16 ounces whipped topping
10 ounces chocolate covered toffee
　bars, coarsely chopped
2 cups pecans, chopped and toasted

To prepare the chocolate mousse, sprinkle the gelatin over the cold water in a bowl. Let stand to soften for 2 minutes. Add the boiling water and stir until the gelatin is dissolved and the mixture is clear. Let cool slightly.

Mix the sugar and cocoa in a large mixing bowl. Add the whipping cream and vanilla. Beat at medium speed until firm peaks form, scraping down the side occasionally. Add the gelatin mixture and beat well. Chill, covered, until ready to assemble the trifle.

To assemble the trifle, break the brownies into bite-size pieces. Layer a single layer of the brownie pieces, the chocolate syrup, the chocolate mousse, the whipped topping, the candy bars and the pecans one-half at a time in a trifle dish. There may be some extra brownie pieces. Chill, covered, 8 to 10 hours. Prepared chocolate mousse mix may be substituted for the homemade chocolate mousse.

Serves 10 to 12

He who eats till he is sick must fast till he is well.

Hebrew Proverb

Spanish Flan Dessert

8 eggs
$2/3$ cup sugar
1 (12-ounce) can evaporated milk
1 cup low-fat milk
$1/2$ cup water
1 teaspoon vanilla extract
$1/3$ cup sugar
1 tablespoon water

Beat the eggs and $2/3$ cup sugar in a mixing bowl until smooth. Add the evaporated milk, low-fat milk, $1/2$ cup water and the vanilla. Beat until smooth. Mix $1/3$ cup sugar and 1 tablespoon water in a saucepan. Cook until a rich golden brown and smooth, stirring frequently. Remove from the heat and immediately pour into a 10-inch cake pan. Tilt and rotate the cake pan to coat the bottom and the side of the pan evenly. Pour the egg mixture over the caramel immediately. Place the cake pan in a larger baking pan. Add very hot water to the baking pan to come halfway up the side of the cake pan. Bake at 350 degrees for 45 minutes or until a knife inserted in the center comes out clean. Let cool completely. Chill, covered with foil, for 2 to 3 hours.

To serve, run a sharp knife along the edge of the flan. Dip the cake pan in 1 inch hot water for 10 to 20 seconds. Dry the bottom of the cake pan. Invert onto a 12-inch serving plate. Garnish with sliced fresh fruit or dollops of whipped cream.

Serves 8

In a broken nest there are few whole eggs.

Chinese Proverb

Passover Cake

Cake
1/4 cup blanched whole almonds
3 tablespoons matzo cake meal
9 ounces bittersweet chocolate or
    semisweet chocolate, chopped
1 cup (2 sticks) unsalted butter
6 egg whites
1/3 cup granulated sugar
6 egg yolks
1/3 cup packed light brown sugar

1/3 cup granulated sugar
1 1/2 teaspoons grated orange zest
1/8 teaspoon salt
1/4 cup confectioners' sugar (optional)

Raspberry Sauce
1 (10-to 12-ounce) package frozen
    raspberries, thawed
2 to 4 tablespoons water
3 to 4 tablespoons sugar

To prepare the cake, process the almonds and cake meal in a food processor fitted with a steel blade until finely ground. Combine the chocolate and butter in a microwave-safe bowl. Microwave at 50 percent for 30-second intervals until melted, stirring well after each interval. Let stand to cool slightly. Beat the egg whites in a mixing bowl at medium speed for 2 minutes or until foamy. Add 1/3 cup granulated sugar gradually, beating constantly at high speed until stiff peaks form.

Combine the egg yolks, brown sugar, 1/3 cup granulated sugar, the orange zest and salt in a mixing bowl. Beat at high speed for 2 minutes or until pale yellow and thick. Add the chocolate mixture gradually, beating constantly at low speed. Stir in the almond mixture and one-fourth of the egg white mixture. Fold in the remaining egg white mixture. Spoon into an ungreased springform pan. Bake at 375 degrees for 35 to 40 minutes or until a wooden pick inserted 1 1/2 inches from the side comes out almost clean. The top may crack. Cool in the pan on a wire rack.

To prepare the sauce, purée the undrained raspberries and 2 tablespoons water in a blender. Add additional water as needed to thin the mixture enough to pass through a fine wire mesh strainer. Press through the strainer into a saucepan, scraping the underside of the strainer with a rubber spatula. Discard the solids. Add the sugar. Bring to a boil over medium heat. Boil gently for 3 minutes. Remove from the heat and pour into a small pitcher. Serve hot or chill, covered, until serving time.

To serve, run a sharp knife around the edge of the cake. Remove the side of the pan. Slice the cake and place on dessert plates. Drizzle with the raspberry sauce. Sprinkle with the confectioners' sugar when serving for occasions other than Passover.

Serves 12

Baba

Pastry
2 cups sifted all-purpose flour
2 tablespoons baking powder
2 eggs
1/2 cup sugar
1/2 cup (1 stick) butter, softened
1/3 cup (about) milk

Baba
1 cup granulated sugar
1/2 cup cornstarch

Pinch of salt
4 cups milk
7 egg yolks
1 tablespoon butter
2 teaspoons vanilla extract
2 cups freshly grated coconut or
　　shredded coconut
7 egg whites
3/4 teaspoon cream of tartar
1/2 cup confectioners' sugar

To prepare the pastry, sift the flour and baking powder together. Beat 2 eggs and 1/2 cup sugar in a bowl until light and creamy. Add the butter and beat until combined. Add the sifted ingredients and 1/3 cup milk. Beat until a soft dough forms. Wrap the dough in plastic wrap. Chill for 1 hour. Roll out on a lightly floured surface and fit into a lightly greased 10×15-inch baking pan. Bake at 350 degrees for 12 to 15 minutes or until light brown. Let stand to cool.

To prepare the baba, combine 1 cup granulated sugar, the cornstarch and salt in a large glass bowl. Heat 4 cups milk in a small heavy saucepan over low heat to just below a boil, stirring constantly. Add to the sugar mixture gradually, stirring constantly. Place the bowl over simmering water. (Do not allow the water to touch the bottom of the bowl.) Cook until thickened, stirring occasionally. Beat the egg yolks lightly in a bowl. Stir one-third of the hot milk mixture into the egg yolks to temper, and then stir the egg yolks into the remaining milk mixture. Cook for 3 minutes, stirring constantly. Remove from the heat and stir in the butter and vanilla. Let stand to cool slightly. Spread over the pastry and sprinkle with the coconut. Beat the egg whites with the cream of tartar in a mixing bowl until soft peaks form. Add the confectioners' sugar gradually, beating until stiff peaks form. Spread over the coconut. Bake at 350 degrees for 6 minutes or until the meringue is golden brown. Let stand to cool. Cut into squares.

Serves 15

Happy are those who hunger and thirst for what is right; they shall be satisfied.

Matthew 5:6

No-Bake Cake

1/2 cup (1 stick) butter, softened
8 ounces cream cheese, softened
2 cups confectioners' sugar
1 (20-ounce) can crushed
   pineapple

1 (7-ounce) can shredded coconut
1 cup chopped nuts
1 (12-ounce) package vanilla wafers
8 to 12 ounces whipped topping
1/2 cup chopped nuts

Beat the butter and cream cheese in a large mixing bowl until smooth. Add the confectioners' sugar and beat until light and fluffy. Stir in the pineapple, coconut and 1 cup nuts. Layer the vanilla wafers and pineapple mixture one-half at a time in a 9×13-inch dish. Spread the whipped topping over the top. Chill, covered for 8 to 10 hours. Sprinkle with 1/2 cup nuts before serving.

Serves 12 to 15

If you wish to go to extremes, let it be in sweetness, patience, humility, and charity.

St. Phillip Neri

Strawberry Tiramisu

1 1/2 pounds strawberries
2/3 cup granulated sugar
2 1/2 teaspoons almond extract
16 ounces mascarpone
   cheese, softened

1 3/4 cups heavy whipping cream
2/3 cup confectioners' sugar
24 to 28 savoiardi cookies
   (thick crisp ladyfingers)
2 ounces semisweet chocolate, grated

Process the strawberries, granulated sugar and almond extract in a blender until smooth; set aside. Beat the mascarpone cheese in a mixing bowl for 30 seconds. Add the whipping cream. Beat at high speed for 2 minutes. Scrape down the side of the bowl. Beat until stiff peaks form. Add the confectioners' sugar 2 tablespoons at a time, beating well after each addition. Layer the cookies, strawberry mixture and cheese mixture one-half at a time in a 9×9-inch dish. Trim the cookies as needed to fit tightly in a single layer. Chill, covered with plastic wrap, for 8 to 10 hours. Sprinkle with the chocolate and cut into squares.

Serves 12

Meringue Shells with Fresh Berries

3 egg whites
1/4 teaspoon cream of tartar
1 cup granulated sugar
3/4 cup crushed butter crackers
1/2 cup pecans, chopped
4 cups fresh mixed berries
   (strawberries, blackberries
   and blueberries)

2 tablespoons Grand Marnier
4 packets artificial sweetener, or
   to taste
Sweetened whipped cream or
   whipped topping

Beat the egg whites with the cream of tartar in a mixing bowl until stiff peaks form. Add the sugar 1 tablespoon at a time, beating constantly until stiff peaks form. Fold in the crackers and pecans. Line two baking sheets with baking parchment. Spread or pipe into fifteen 4- to 5-inch discs on the prepared baking sheets, making the outer edge taller than the center. Bake at 250 to 275 degrees for 1 hour or until crisp. Cool on the baking sheets. Mash the berries in a bowl. Stir in the liqueur and artificial sweetener. Chill, covered, until serving time. To serve, place the meringue shells on dessert plates. Spoon the berry mixture into the center of the shells. Top each with a dollop of the whipped cream.

Serves 15

Strawberry Flambé

1/2 cup (1 stick) margarine
1 cup packed light brown sugar
1 pound strawberries, cut into
   quarters

1 to 2 teaspoons lemon extract
Pinch of cinnamon
2 to 4 tablespoons rum
Vanilla ice cream

Combine the margarine and brown sugar in a skillet. Cook over medium heat until the margarine melts and the sugar is dissolved, stirring frequently. Add the strawberries and cook until tender, stirring occasionally. Stir in the lemon extract and cinnamon. Pour the rum over the mixture and remove from the heat. Ignite the rum carefully. Let flame briefly before stirring to extinguish. Serve over vanilla ice cream.

Serves 12

Chocolate Chunk Butter Pecan Ice Cream

2 cups 2% milk
1 cup heavy whipping cream
1 (12-ounce) can evaporated milk
1 cup sugar
1 (3-ounce) package vanilla instant pudding mix
1 teaspoon vanilla extract
1 tablespoon butter
1 cup pecans, chopped
1 cup coarsely chopped chocolate

Combine the milk, cream, evaporated milk, sugar, pudding mix and vanilla in a large pitcher. Stir until the sugar and pudding mix are dissolved. Chill, covered. Melt the butter in a heavy skillet. Add the pecans and cook until light brown, stirring frequently. Drain on paper towels. Pour the milk mixture into a well chilled ice cream freezer container. Stir in the pecans and chocolate. Freeze using the manufacturer's directions.

Makes 1 quart

Because of the abundance of brown pelicans found along the coast of Louisiana, the state is commonly referred to as "The Pelican State." This bird has been a symbol of Louisiana since the arrival of early European settlers who were impressed with the pelican's generous and nurturing attitude toward their young.

Fresh Apple Cake

Cake
2 1/2 cups all-purpose flour
2 teaspoons baking powder
1 teaspoon baking soda
1 teaspoon salt
1 teaspoon cinnamon
1 teaspoon ground nutmeg
1 cup canola oil
2 cups sugar
3 eggs, beaten
1 teaspoon vanilla extract

4 cups apples, peeled and chopped
1 cup pecans, chopped

Vanilla Cream Cheese Frosting
1 (1-pound) package confectioners' sugar, sifted
8 ounces cream cheese, softened
1/2 cup butter (1 stick), softened
2 teaspoons vanilla extract
1 cup chopped pecans

Sift the flour, baking powder, baking soda, salt, cinnamon and nutmeg together. Mix the canola oil and sugar in a bowl. Add the eggs and mix until smooth. Add the sifted dry ingredients and mix well. Fold in the vanilla, apples and pecans. Pour into a greased and floured 9×13-inch cake pan. Bake at 325 degrees for 55 minutes. Let cool completely.

To prepare the frosting, cream the sugar, cream cheese and butter in a mixing bowl at low speed until light and fluffy. Stir in the vanilla and pecans. Spread the frosting over the top of the cake.

Serves 15

Keep me as the apple of your eye.

Psalm 17:8a

Coca-Cola Cake

Cake

2 cups all-purpose flour
$^{1}/_{4}$ cup baking cocoa
1 teaspoon baking soda
1 cup Coca-Cola
$^{1}/_{2}$ cup buttermilk
$^{1}/_{3}$ cup canola oil
$1^{3}/_{4}$ cups sugar
1 egg
1 teaspoon vanilla extract
$1^{1}/_{2}$ cups miniature marshmallows

Coca-Cola Chocolate Frosting

6 tablespoons butter
$^{1}/_{3}$ cup Coca-Cola
$^{1}/_{4}$ cup baking cocoa
1 (1-pound) package
   confectioners' sugar
1 teaspoon vanilla extract

To prepare the cake, mix the flour, baking cocoa and baking soda together. Mix the cola and buttermilk in a small bowl. Beat the canola oil, sugar, egg and vanilla in a mixing bowl until smooth and creamy. Add the dry ingredients and the cola mixture alternately, mixing well after each addition. Stir in the marshmallows. Spread into a 9×13-inch cake pan sprayed with nonstick cooking spray. Bake at 350 degrees for 35 minutes or until a wooden skewer inserted into the center of the cake comes out clean.

To prepare the frosting, combine the butter, cola and baking cocoa in a saucepan. Bring to a boil, stirring frequently. Remove from the heat and stir in the confectioners' sugar and vanilla. Pour over the warm cake. Let cool completely before serving.

Serves 14 to 16

This recipe was graciously donated to us by Holly Clegg. She created this recipe for the 100th Anniversary of the Baton Rouge Coca-Cola Bottling Company.

King Cake

Cake
2 cups sour cream
$^1/3$ cup sugar
$^1/4$ cup ($^1/2$ stick) butter
1 teaspoon salt
$^1/2$ cup water
2 envelopes dry yeast
1 tablespoon sugar
2 eggs, lightly beaten
$6^1/2$ cups bread flour
Purple, green and gold sparkling sugar sprinkles
Cream cheese, softened (optional)

Cinnamon Filling (optional)
$^1/3$ cup butter, softened
$^1/2$ cup sugar
2 teaspoons cinnamon

Glaze
3 cups confectioners' sugar
3 tablespoons butter, melted
$^1/4$ teaspoon vanilla extract
4 to 6 tablespoons milk

To prepare the cake, combine the sour cream, $^1/3$ cup sugar, the butter and salt in a medium saucepan. Heat over low heat until the butter melts and the mixture is smooth, stirring frequently. Set aside to cool to 100 to 110 degrees. Heat the water in a saucepan to 100 to 110 degrees. Dissolve the yeast and 1 tablespoon sugar in the warm water. Let stand for 5 minutes.

Combine the sour cream mixture, yeast mixture, eggs and 2 cups of the flour in a mixing bowl. Beat at medium speed until smooth. Add the remaining 4^1/$_2$ cups flour gradually, beating constantly on low speed until a soft dough forms. Knead on a lightly floured surface for 10 minutes or until smooth and elastic. Place in a greased bowl, turning to coat the surface. Let rise, covered, in a warm place (about 85 degrees) away from drafts for 1 hour or until the dough has doubled in bulk. Punch the dough down and divide into halves.

To prepare the cinnamon filling, mix the butter, sugar and cinnamon in a bowl. Roll each portion of dough into a 12×22-inch rectangle. Spread with cream cheese or the cinnamon mixture leaving a 1-inch border. Roll from the long side. Place seam side down on greased baking sheets. Shape each into a ring. Moisten the ends with water and pinch to seal. Let rise, covered, in a warm place (about 85 degrees) away from drafts for 20 to 30 minutes or until the dough has doubled in bulk. Bake at 375 degrees for 14 to 16 minutes or until golden brown. Cool on the baking sheets on a wire rack for 10 minutes.

To prepare the glaze, mix the confectioners' sugar, butter and vanilla together in a bowl. Add the milk 2 tablespoons at a time, mixing well after each addition until of a spreading consistency. Spread over the warm cakes. Sprinkle immediately with sugar sprinkles, alternating the colors in bands. Let cool completely before serving.

Serves 36

The King Cake tradition came to New Orleans with the French settlers around 1870, continuing a custom dating back to twelfth-century France.

Cranberry Upside-Down Cake

Cake
1 tablespoon all-purpose flour
1 cup fresh or frozen cranberries
1/2 cup coarsely chopped pitted dates
1/2 cup walnuts, chopped
1 tablespoon grated orange zest
2 tablespoons butter, softened
1/2 cup packed light brown sugar
2 tablespoons orange juice
1/2 teaspoon cinnamon
1 1/2 cups all-purpose flour
1 teaspoon baking powder

1/2 teaspoon salt
6 tablespoons butter, softened
1 cup granulated sugar
1 egg, at room temperature
1 teaspoon vanilla extract
1/2 cup low-fat buttermilk

Glaze
1 cup confectioners' sugar
2 tablespoons orange juice
1 teaspoon butter, melted

Spray a 9×9-inch cake pan with nonstick cooking spray. Dust with 1 tablespoon flour, discarding any excess. Combine the cranberries, dates, walnuts and orange zest in a bowl. Melt 2 tablespoons butter in a saucepan over medium heat. Stir in the brown sugar, orange juice and cinnamon. Cook for 3 minutes, stirring constantly. Pour into the prepared pan. Sprinkle with the cranberry mixture. Mix 1 1/2 cups flour, the baking powder and salt together. Cream 6 tablespoons butter and the granulated sugar in a mixing bowl at medium speed until light and fluffy. Add the egg and vanilla and beat until smooth. Add the flour mixture and buttermilk alternately, beginning and ending with the flour mixture and mixing well after each addition. Spoon over the cranberry mixture.

Bake at 350 degrees for 40 minutes or until a wooden skewer inserted into the center comes out clean. Cool in the baking pan on a wire rack for 5 minutes. Run a sharp knife along the edges of the cake and invert onto a serving plate.

To prepare the glaze, mix the confectioners' sugar, orange juice and butter in a bowl until smooth. Drizzle over the warm cake. Let cool completely before serving.

Serves 12

Eat honey, my son, since it is good; honey that drips from the comb is sweet to the taste.

Proverbs 24:13

Pecan Date Fruitcake

1 cup all-purpose flour
1 cup sugar
1/2 teaspoon baking powder
1/2 teaspoon salt
2 pounds pitted dates, cut into quarters
1 pound pecan halves (about 4 cups)
1 pound candied cherries, cut into halves
4 eggs
2 teaspoons vanilla extract

Line three greased 4×8-inch loaf pans with waxed paper or greased baking parchment. Mix the flour, sugar, baking powder and salt in a bowl. Fold in the dates, pecans and cherries, coating well. Beat the eggs and vanilla in a mixing bowl until foamy. Fold in the date mixture. Divide among the prepared pans.

Bake at 300 degrees for 1 hour or until a wooden skewer inserted into the center comes out clean. Cool in the pans for 10 minutes. Remove to a wire rack and remove the waxed paper. Let cool completely. Wrap tightly with foil and store in a cool dry place until serving time.

Serves 36

He then distributed among all the people, to each man and each woman in the entire multitude of Israel, a loaf of bread, a cut of roast meat, and a raisin cake. With this, all people left for their homes.

2 Samuel 6:19

Louisiana Lagniappe's Pecan Pie

1/2 cup (1 stick) butter
1 cup dark corn syrup
1 cup packed light brown sugar
3 eggs, beaten
1/2 teaspoon lemon juice
1 teaspoon vanilla extract
Pinch of salt
1 cup coarsely chopped pecans
1 unbaked (9-inch) pie shell

Brown the butter in a saucepan. Remove from the heat. Combine the corn syrup, brown sugar, eggs, lemon juice, vanilla and salt in a bowl. Mix until smooth. Stir in the pecans and browned butter. Pour into the pie shell. Bake at 425 degrees for 10 minutes. Reduce the oven temperature to 325 degrees. Bake for 40 to 45 minutes longer or until the center is firm. Let cool completely before serving.

Serves 6 to 8

Lagniappe (pronounced LAN-yap) means "something extra." Lagniappe is composed of the French word la, *meaning "the," and the French adaptation of the Spanish word* napa, *"a present made to a customer." Louisiana Lagniappe Restaurant, located near Baton Rouge, is dedicated to providing its customers the freshest seafood and prime steak available.*

Pecan Cheesecake Pie

8 ounces cream cheese, softened
1 egg, lightly beaten
$1/2$ cup sugar
1 teaspoon vanilla extract
$1/4$ teaspoon salt
1 unbaked (9-inch) pie shell

$1^1/4$ cups chopped pecans
1 cup light corn syrup
3 eggs, lightly beaten
$1/4$ cup sugar
1 teaspoon vanilla extract
Sweetened whipped cream

Beat the cream cheese, 1 egg, $1/2$ cup sugar, 1 teaspoon vanilla and the salt in a mixing bowl at medium speed until smooth and creamy. Pour into the pie shell. Sprinkle with the pecans.

Whisk the corn syrup, 3 eggs, $1/4$ cup sugar and 1 teaspoon vanilla in a bowl until smooth and creamy. Pour over the pecans. Place on a baking sheet. Bake at 350 degrees for 55 minutes or until the center is firm. Let cool completely. Serve with sweetened whipped cream.

Serves 8

Chocolate Chess Pie

2 eggs
$1^1/2$ cups sugar
1 (5-ounce) can evaporated milk
$1/2$ cup (1 stick) butter, melted
$1/4$ cup baking cocoa
1 tablespoon all-purpose flour

Pinch of salt
1 teaspoon vanilla extract
1 unbaked (9-inch) pie shell
Whipped cream or ice cream
   (optional)

Beat the eggs and sugar in a mixing bowl until thick and creamy. Add the evaporated milk and butter and mix well. Add the baking cocoa, flour and salt and mix well. Stir in the vanilla and pour into the pie shell. Bake at 350 degrees for 35 to 45 minutes or until the center is firm. Let cool completely. Serve with whipped cream or ice cream.

Serves 8

Feed your faith and your doubts will starve to death.

E. C. McKenzie

Strawberry Chocolate Cream Pie

22 cream-filled chocolate cookies, finely crushed
1/4 cup (1/2 stick) butter, melted
1 teaspoon unflavored gelatin
1 tablespoon cold water
2 tablespoons boiling water
1 cup cold heavy whipping cream
1/2 cup granulated sugar
1/4 cup baking cocoa
1 teaspoon vanilla extract
1 cup chopped strawberries
3/4 cup cold heavy whipping cream
2 to 3 tablespoons confectioners' sugar

Mix the cookies and butter in a bowl. Press over the bottom and up the side of a 9-inch pie plate. Freeze until needed. Sprinkle the gelatin over the cold water in a bowl. Let stand for 2 minutes to soften. Add the boiling water and stir until the gelatin is dissolved and the mixture is clear.

Beat 1 cup whipping cream, the granulated sugar, baking cocoa and vanilla in a chilled mixing bowl until stiff peaks form. Add the gelatin mixture and mix well. Pour into the prepared pie plate. Chill, covered, for 3 to 10 hours. Sprinkle with the strawberries 1 hour before serving. Beat 3/4 cup whipping cream in a mixing bowl until soft peaks form. Add the confectioners' sugar gradually, beating constantly until stiff peaks form. Spread over the strawberries just before serving. Garnish with whole strawberries.

Serves 8

They shared their food gladly and generously; they praised God and were looked up to by everyone.

Acts 2:47

Strawberry Pie

1 quart strawberries
1/2 cup boiling water
1 cup sugar
3 tablespoons cornstarch
1/4 teaspoon salt
3 or 4 drops red food coloring (optional)
1 baked (9-inch) pie shell
8 ounces whipped cream or whipped topping

Mash enough of the strawberries in a bowl to measure 1 cup. Save the prettiest strawberries for the assembly. Combine the mashed strawberries, water, sugar, cornstarch and salt in a saucepan. Cook over medium heat until thickened, stirring constantly. Remove from the heat and add the food coloring. Let cool completely. Place the reserved strawberries into the pie shell and top with the sauce. Decorate with the whipped cream.

Serves 8

Ponchatoula received its motto, Strawberry Capital of the World, because of the many strawberry farms in the area. Ponchatoula derives its name from the Choctaw Indian language meaning "hair to hang" because of the abundance of Spanish moss on the trees surrounding the area.

Praline Pumpkin Pie

$1/3$ cup packed brown sugar
$1/3$ cup chopped pecans
3 tablespoons butter, softened
1 unbaked (9-inch) pie shell
$1^1/2$ cups canned pumpkin
1 cup evaporated milk
$1/2$ cup water
3 eggs, at room temperature
$1/2$ cup packed brown sugar
$1/2$ cup granulated sugar
$1^1/2$ teaspoons pumpkin pie spice
$1/2$ teaspoon salt

Mix $1/3$ cup brown sugar, the pecans and butter in a small bowl. Press firmly over the bottom of the pie shell. Bake at 450 degrees for 10 minutes. Remove from the oven and decrease the oven temperature to 350 degrees. Let the pie shell cool for 10 minutes. Beat the pumpkin, evaporated milk and water in a mixing bowl. Add the eggs one at a time, mixing well after each addition. Add $1/2$ cup brown sugar, the granulated sugar, pumpkin pie spice and salt. Mix until smooth. Pour into the partially baked pie shell. Bake for 45 to 50 minutes or until the center is firm.

Serves 6 to 8

You don't have to cook fancy masterpieces—just good food from fresh ingredients.
Julia Child

Buttermilk Pie

1 unbaked (10-inch) deep-dish pie shell
1/4 cup (1/2 stick) butter, melted
2 cups sugar
11/2 tablespoons all-purpose flour
3 eggs
1 cup buttermilk
Dash of baking soda
2 teaspoons vanilla extract
1/4 to 1/2 teaspoon grated nutmeg (optional)

Line the pie shell with heavy-duty foil and fill with pie weights. Bake at 450 degrees for 8 minutes. Remove the foil and pie weights. Bake for 4 minutes longer. Let cool slightly. Decrease the oven temperature to 350 degrees.

Beat the butter, sugar and flour together in a mixing bowl. Add the eggs one at a time, mixing well after each addition. Mix the buttermilk and baking soda in a small bowl. Stir in the egg mixture. Add the vanilla and pour into the partially baked pie shell. Sprinkle with the nutmeg. Cover the edge of the shell with heavy-duty foil to prevent the crust from burning. Bake for 35 to 40 minutes or until a knife inserted into the center comes out clean. Let cool completely on a wire rack.

Serves 8

Cooking is at once one of the simplest and most gratifying of the arts, but to cook well, one must love and respect food.

Craig Claiborne

Never-Fail Pie Crust

3 cups all-purpose flour
1 teaspoon salt
1¼ cups shortening
¼ cup plus 1 tablespoon water
1 egg, beaten
1 tablespoon vinegar

Mix the flour and salt in a large bowl. Cut in the shortening until crumbly. Mix the water, egg and vinegar in a small bowl. Add to the flour mixture and stir with a spoon until combined. Divide the dough into thirds. Use immediately or wrap each portion tightly with plastic wrap and store in the refrigerator until needed. Let stand at room temperature for 5 to 8 minutes before using.

Roll one portion of the dough on a lightly floured surface to 2 inches larger than the pie plate. Fit into the pie plate, careful not to stretch the dough.

To prepare a one-crust pie, trim the dough to within 1 inch of the pie plate. Roll the overhanging dough under and flute or crimp the edge as desired. For prebaked shells, bake at 450 degrees for 8 to 10 minutes.

To prepare a two-crust pie, fill the pie shell with desired filling and trim the dough to within ½-inch from the pie plate. Roll a second portion of the dough. Fit over the filling. Cut slits in the top for steam to escape. Trim the overhanging dough to within 1 inch of the pie plate. Roll the dough under the lower edge of dough and press to seal. Flute or crimp as desired. Bake according to the pie recipe.

This is an easy crust to handle and can be rerolled as needed without toughening.

Makes 3 (9-inch) crusts

She left and did as Elijah had said. She was able to eat for a year, and he and her son as well; the jar of flour did not go empty, nor did the jug of oil run dry . . .

1 Kings 17:15–16

Divinity Fudge

2 egg whites
3 cups sugar
1/2 cup light corn syrup

1/2 cup boiling water
1 cup pecans, chopped
1 teaspoon vanilla extract

Beat the egg whites in a mixing bowl until stiff peaks form. Combine the sugar, corn syrup and water in a saucepan and mix well. Bring to a boil over medium-high heat. Cook, uncovered, over high heat to 250 to 265 degrees on a candy thermometer, hard-ball stage. Add to the egg whites gradually, beating constantly at low speed until combined. Beat at medium speed until stiff. Add the pecans and vanilla and mix well. Pour into a buttered 9×13-inch pan. Let cool completely and then cut into squares.

Makes 4 dozen

Peanut Butter Fudge

3 cups sugar
3 tablespoons light corn syrup
1/4 teaspoon salt
1 cup milk
3 tablespoons butter

1 1/2 teaspoons vanilla extract
1/3 cup (heaping) peanut butter
2 tablespoons (heaping)
marshmallow creme

Combine the sugar, corn syrup, salt and milk in a heavy 3-quart saucepan. Bring to a boil slowly, stirring frequently. Cook, uncovered, over high heat to 234 to 240 degrees on a candy thermometer, soft-ball stage. Remove from the heat and stir in the butter. Stir in the peanut butter and marshmallow creme. Beat by hand until thick and creamy. Pour into a buttered 8×8-inch baking pan. Let stand until firm. Cut into squares.

Makes 3 dozen

How far you go in life depends on you being tender with the young, compassionate with the aged, sympathetic with the striving and tolerant of the weak and strong. Because someday in your life you will have been all of these.

George Washington Carver

Pralines

1 cup granulated sugar
1 cup packed light brown sugar
3/4 cup half-and-half
1/4 teaspoon salt

1 cup chopped pecans
3 tablespoons butter
1 teaspoon vanilla extract

Combine the granulated sugar, brown sugar, half-and-half and salt in a greased 2-quart saucepan. Cook over low heat for 6 minutes or until the sugar is dissolved, stirring constantly. Increase the heat to medium and cook for 10 minutes or until the mixture comes to a boil. Reduce the heat to medium-low and cook for 15 minutes longer or to 234 to 240 degrees on a candy thermometer, soft-ball stage. Remove from the heat. Add the pecans, butter and vanilla. Do not stir. Let stand for 5 minutes. Beat with a wooden spoon for 2 to 3 minutes or until the mixture thickens and looses its luster. Drop the mixture by spoonfuls onto greased waxed paper, working quickly. If the mixture becomes too thick, stir in hot water, 1/2 teaspoon at a time, until the mixture reaches the desired consistency. Let stand until cool. Store in an airtight container.

Makes 30

The first pralines were made in seventeenth-century France and consisted of whole almonds coated in caramelized sugar. The Creoles substituted pecans for the almonds. Pralines became a part of Louisiana food culture as early as 1762.

Creamy Pralines

1 cup granulated sugar
1/2 cup packed light brown sugar
1/2 cup packed dark brown sugar
1/2 cup (1 stick) butter

1/2 cup evaporated milk
16 large marshmallows
2 cups chopped pecans, toasted
2 teaspoons rum flavoring

Mix the granulated sugar, brown sugars, butter and evaporated milk in a 2-quart saucepan. Cook over medium heat until 250 to 265 degrees on a candy thermometer, hard-ball stage. Remove from the heat and stir in the marshmallows, pecans and rum flavoring. Stir until the mixture thickens and looses its luster. Drop by spoonfuls onto waxed paper. Let stand until cool. Store in an airtight container.

Makes 24

Peanut Brittle

1 cup raw peanuts
1 cup sugar
$1/3$ cup light corn syrup
$1/3$ cup water

1 teaspoon butter
1 teaspoon vanilla extract
1 teaspoon baking soda

Combine the peanuts, sugar, corn syrup, water and butter in a heavy 3-quart saucepan. Cook over medium-high to 300 to 310 degrees on a candy thermometer, hard-crack stage. Remove from the heat and stir in the vanilla and baking soda. Stir until the mixture stops foaming. Pour into a buttered 9×13-inch baking pan. Let cool completely. Invert onto waxed paper and break into pieces. Store in an airtight container.

Serves 10 to 12

Barukh ata Adonai, Eloheinu, Melekh ha olam, bo're minei m'zonot.
Blessed are You, LORD, our God, King of the universe, who creates varieties of nourishment.

Jewish Blessing Prayer

Chocolate Toffee Bars

15 graham crackers
1 cup (2 sticks) butter
1 cup light brown sugar

2 cups toasted pecans, chopped
1 teaspoon vanilla extract
12 ounces semisweet chocolate chips

Line a greased 10×15-inch baking pan with the graham crackers. Combine the butter, brown sugar and pecans in a saucepan. Bring the mixture to a boil and boil for 1 minute. Remove from the heat and stir in the vanilla. Pour over the graham crackers. Bake at 350 degrees for 12 minutes. Sprinkle immediately with the chocolate chips. Spread with an offset spatula. Freeze until firm. Break into pieces. Store in an airtight container.

Serves 20

To eat too much honey is not good; nor to seek honor after honor.

Proverbs 25:27

167

Macadamia Nut and White Chocolate Cookies

2 1/2 cups all-purpose flour
1 teaspoon baking soda
1/2 teaspoon salt
3/4 cup (1 1/2 sticks) unsalted butter, softened
1 cup packed light brown sugar
3/4 cup granulated sugar
2 eggs, at room temperature
1 teaspoon vanilla extract
11 ounces white chocolate chips
1 1/2 cups macadamia nuts, chopped

Sift the flour, baking soda and salt together. Beat the butter in a mixing bowl at low speed for 30 to 45 seconds or until creamy. Add the brown sugar and granulated sugar gradually, beating constantly until light and fluffy. Add the eggs one at a time, beating well after each addition. Add the vanilla and mix well. Stir in the flour mixture with a wooden spoon. Stir in the white chocolate chips and macadamia nuts.

Drop by rounded tablespoonfuls 1 inch apart onto baking parchment-lined cookie sheets. Flatten each slightly. Bake at 350 degrees for 10 to 12 minutes or until the edges are light brown and the centers are still soft. Cool on the cookie sheets for 3 to 4 minutes. Remove to a wire rack to cool completely.

Makes 3 dozen

A good tree cannot bear bad fruit, nor can a rotten tree bear good fruit.

Shade Tree Oatmeal Cookies

3 cups all-purpose flour
2 teaspoons baking soda
2 teaspoons salt
2 cups (4 sticks) cold butter, finely chopped
2 (1-pound) packages dark brown sugar
4 eggs, lightly beaten
3 tablespoons molasses
2 teaspoons vanilla extract
1 (15-ounce) package golden raisins
4 cups coarsely chopped pecans
6 cups rolled oats

Sift the flour, baking soda and salt. Mix the butter, brown sugar, eggs, molasses and vanilla in a bowl. Stir in the sifted dry ingredients. Add the raisins, pecans and oats in the order listed, mixing well after each addition. Divide the dough into six equal portions. Chill, covered, for 1 hour. Roll each portion into a log. Wrap tightly in plastic wrap and place in a sealable plastic freezer bag. Freeze until baking time.

Slice each frozen log of dough into twelve slices. Arrange on a greased or baking parchment-lined cookie sheet. Bake at 350 degrees for 13 minutes. Remove from the cookie sheet immediately to a wire rack to cool. The cookies will set as they cool.

Makes 6 dozen

Do not work for food that perishes but for food that endures for eternal life, which the Son of Man will give you.

John 6:27a

Holiday Oatmeal Cookies

2 cups all-purpose flour
1 teaspoon baking soda
$^1/_2$ teaspoon baking powder
$^1/_2$ teaspoon salt
1 cup (2 sticks) butter or margarine, softened
1 cup packed light brown sugar
$^1/_2$ cup granulated sugar
1 egg
2 teaspoons vanilla extract
2 cups sweetened dried cranberries
1$^1/_2$ cups pecans, toasted and chopped
1$^1/_4$ cups quick-cooking oats
12 ounces dark chocolate baking squares or white chocolate (optional)
3 tablespoons shortening (optional)

Combine the flour, baking soda, baking powder and salt. Beat the butter in a mixing bowl until creamy. Add the brown sugar and granulated sugar. Beat until light and fluffy. Add the egg and vanilla and mix well. Add the dry ingredients and mix well. Stir in the cranberries, pecans and oats. The dough will be sticky. Drop by rounded tablespoonfuls onto lightly greased cookie sheets. Bake at 350 degrees for 10 minutes or until light brown. Remove to a wire rack to cool.

Combine the chocolate and shortening in a microwave-safe bowl. Microwave on Medium at 15-second intervals until the chocolate is melted and the mixture is smooth, stirring after each interval. Dip half of each cookie into the chocolate mixture and place on waxed paper. Let stand until the chocolate is firm.

Makes 4 dozen

To live the Eucharist is the secret of bringing God to the world and of leading the world to God.

Cardinal Francis Xavier Nguyen Van Thuan

Coconut Mounds

2 eggs
1 cup sugar
1 teaspoon vanilla extract
14 ounces (or more) sweetened flaked coconut
1/4 cup sifted all-purpose flour
1 cup (6 ounces) semisweet chocolate chips (optional)
1 tablespoon shortening (optional)

Combine the eggs, sugar and vanilla in a mixing bowl. Beat at high speed for 1 minute. Fold in the coconut and flour. If the mixture is too thin add additional coconut. Drop by slightly mounded tablespoonfuls 2 inches apart onto a lightly greased or baking parchment-lined cookie sheet. Bake at 350 degrees for 15 to 18 minutes or until golden brown. Remove from the cookie sheet immediately to a wire rack to cool.

Combine the chocolate chips and shortening in a microwave-safe bowl. Microwave on Medium at 15-second intervals until the chocolate is melted and the mixture is smooth, stirring after each interval. Dip the bottom of the cookies in the chocolate mixture and place chocolate side up on the wire rack. Let stand until the chocolate is firm. Store in an airtight container.

Makes about 2 dozen

LSU Indian Mounds were built by Native Americans more than 5,000 years ago, approximately 450 years before the construction of the great Egyptian pyramids. To date, archaeologists do not know the exact purpose of the mounds, but the structures do not appear to have been burial places, temples, or houses.

Peppermint Biscotti

3 1/4 cups all-purpose flour
1 teaspoon baking powder
1/4 teaspoon salt
3/4 cup (1 1/2 sticks) butter, softened
3/4 cup sugar
3 eggs
2 1/4 teaspoons peppermint extract
1 1/4 cups crushed peppermint candies
2 cups (12 ounces) semisweet chocolate chips (optional)
2 tablespoons shortening (optional)
1/4 teaspoon peppermint extract (optional)

Mix the flour, baking powder and salt together. Cream the butter and sugar in a mixing bowl until light and fluffy. Add the eggs one at a time, beating well after each addition. Add 2 1/4 teaspoons peppermint extract and the candies and mix well. Add the dry ingredients gradually, beating constantly. Divide the dough into halves. Shape each half into a 2 1/2×12-inch rectangle and place on a cookie sheet. Bake at 350 degrees for 25 to 30 minutes or until golden brown. Maintain the oven temperature. Cool on a wire rack for 15 minutes. Remove to a cutting board and slice diagonally into 1/2-inch-thick pieces. Arrange on the cookie sheet. Bake for 15 to 18 minutes or until firm. Cool on a wire rack.

Combine the chocolate chips, shortening and peppermint extract in a microwave-safe bowl. Microwave on Medium for 1 minute and mix well. Microwave at 15-second intervals until the chocolate is melted and the mixture is smooth, stirring after each interval. Let stand for 5 minutes. Dip one end of each cookie into the chocolate mixture and place on waxed paper. Let stand until the chocolate is firm. Store in an airtight container.

Makes about 3 1/2 dozen

They went as a body to the temple every day but met in their houses for the breaking of the bread; they shared their food gladly and generously.

Acts 2:46

Large Quantities

Manna Givers

Manna Givers are groups of volunteers who provide suppers for the guests at our Bishop Ott Shelters. They cook a meal at home, take it to the shelter, serve the shelter guests a family-style supper, and then sit with them enjoying the meal while they visit. The food nourishes their bodies, while the visiting connects seemingly disparate but equally beloved members of the body of Christ, nourishing the spirits of the guests and volunteers alike. The following story illustrates what it means to be a Manna Giver.

"In my enthusiasm as a new Manna Givers volunteer, I had gotten in over my head by saying I'd cook a main dish as well as a dessert. That day, my kitchen was in a state of chaos. To top it all off, it was a hot, humid Louisiana day. I was frazzled and frustrated, and when my fellow volunteers picked me up, I announced that I would never do this again!

"Once we arrived at the shelter, we met the residents and ended up having a pleasant meal together. After dinner, when we were packing up to leave, one of the men came up to me with his empty bowl in his hands. He was crying, weeping openly. He asked if I was the lady who had made the banana pudding. Through his tears, he thanked me and told me that it tasted just like his mother used to make. Seeing this man, restored for a few minutes to his childhood, moved me in a way I was unprepared for. Crying along with him, I told him I would make banana pudding again and bring it to him.

"The man whose mother made banana pudding like mine brought the heart of this ministry home to me: because he shared his hurt and his heart with me, I was able to see clearly the face of Christ crying through him. Until he moved on, I brought him banana pudding every week at the shelter, but what he gave me over the course of those few weeks, allowing me to be Christ to him, was by far the more generous gift."

Manna Givers Volunteer

Pasta e Fagioli Soup

3 pounds ground sirloin or
 ground chuck
2 tablespoons olive oil
2 large onions, chopped
4 or 5 garlic cloves, chopped
2 cups chopped cabbage
3 or 4 ribs celery, chopped
2 or 3 carrots, chopped
1 (28-ounce) can chopped tomatoes
1 bay leaf
1 tablespoon dried basil
1 tablespoon dried oregano
1 tablespoon chopped Italian parsley
2 tablespoons sugar

48 ounces tomato juice cocktail or
 tomato juice
1 (10-ounce) can beef broth
2 (15-ounce) cans white kidney
 beans, drained and rinsed
1 (15-ounce) can Great Northern
 beans, drained and rinsed
1 (15-ounce) can garbanzo beans,
 drained and rinsed
1 cup fresh or frozen green beans
Salt and pepper to taste
3/4 cup uncooked noodles
Grated Parmesan cheese to taste

Brown the ground beef in the olive oil in a large saucepan or stockpot. Drain and return to the skillet. Add the onions and garlic and cook until the onions are tender, stirring occasionally. Add the cabbage, celery and carrots. Cook for 10 to 15 minutes, stirring occasionally. Stir in the tomatoes, bay leaf, basil, oregano, parsley and sugar. Cook for 10 minutes. Stir in the tomato juice cocktail, broth, kidney beans, Great Northern beans, garbanzo beans and green beans. Reduce the heat to medium-low and simmer for 30 minutes, stirring occasionally. Season with salt and pepper. Stir in the pasta and simmer for 7 minutes or until the pasta is tender. Remove and discard the bay leaf. Ladle into soup bowls and top with grated Parmesan cheese. Add additional broth for a thinner consistency.

Serves 12

"Learned good things about myself."

Female Guest, Age 35

Chicken and Pork Jambalaya

8 pounds hot pork sausage, sliced
8 pounds lean pork roast, finely
  chopped
8 pounds boneless chicken, chopped
10 pounds yellow onions, chopped
2 1/2 pounds green bell
  peppers, chopped
2 1/2 pounds red bell peppers, chopped
2 1/2 pounds celery, chopped
2 (10-ounce) cans Rotel chopped
  tomatoes with green chiles
32 cups water

1/2 cup salt
2 tablespoons black pepper
2 tablespoons red pepper
1/4 cup garlic powder
1/2 cup Creole seasoning
2 (4-ounce) bottles browning and
  seasoning sauce (optional)
4 bay leaves
10 pounds long grain rice
2 bunches parsley, chopped
4 bunches green onions, chopped

Cook the sausage in a 5-gallon cast-iron pot or large stockpot for 45 minutes, stirring occasionally. Remove the sausage with a slotted spoon to colander to drain, reserving the drippings in the stockpot. Add the pork to the reserved drippings and cook for 1 hour or until tender, stirring occasionally. Remove with a slotted spoon to a colander to drain, reserving the drippings in the stockpot. Add the chicken to the reserved drippings and cook for 15 minutes, stirring occasionally. Remove the chicken with a slotted spoon to a colander to drain, reserving the drippings in the stockpot. Add the onions, green bell peppers, red bell peppers, celery and tomatoes with green chiles to the reserved drippings. Cook for 1 hour, stirring occasionally.

Return the sausage, pork and chicken to the stockpot and simmer for 10 minutes. Stir in the water, salt, black pepper, red pepper, garlic powder, Creole seasoning, seasoning sauce and bay leaves. Simmer for 30 minutes, skimming the top as needed. Bring to a boil and stir in the rice. Cook until almost all of the liquid is absorbed, stirring occasionally. Cook, covered, on low heat for 25 minutes. Fluff the rice and stir in the parsley and green onions. Cook, covered, for 15 minutes or until the rice is tender.

Serves 50

"They blessed me with a place to stay."
Female Guest, Age 24

Mexican Chicken Stew

1 cup olive oil
4 onions, coarsely chopped
16 garlic cloves, coarsely chopped
8 jalapeño chiles, seeded and sliced
1/4 cup dried oregano
4 teaspoons dried cumin
4 (28-ounce) cans chopped tomatoes
16 cups shredded cooked chicken (about 5 pounds)
3 dashes of Worcestershire sauce
16 cups chicken stock
4 cups cooked white rice
Salt to taste

Heat the olive oil in a large stockpot over medium heat. Add the onions and sauté for 4 to 5 minutes. Add the garlic and jalapeño chiles. Sauté for 8 minutes or until the vegetables are tender. Add the oregano and cumin and cook for 1 to 2 minutes, stirring occasionally. Stir in the tomatoes, chicken, Worcestershire sauce and stock. Bring to a boil, stirring occasionally. Reduce the heat to medium-low and simmer for 20 minutes. Stir in the rice and cook for 5 minutes or until the rice is heated through. Season with salt. Ladle into bowls and garnish with sour cream, chopped fresh cilantro and shredded cheese.

Serves 30

"This program has made my faith in the Lord stronger. The stronger my faith gets the easier everything else gets. I've kept my job and I'm still working and paying my bills."

Male Guest, Age 40

Mushroom Chicken for a Crowd

20 pounds chicken thighs
1/4 cup lemon pepper
2 tablespoons paprika
4 large onions, thinly sliced
3 (26-ounce) cans cream of mushroom soup

Trim the excess fat from the chicken. Arrange the chicken in large roasting pans. Sprinkle evenly with the lemon pepper. Sprinkle evenly with the paprika. Arrange the onions over the chicken. Spread the soup evenly over the onions.

Bake, covered, at 350 degrees for 1 hour. Bake, uncovered, for 1 hour or until the meat begins to pull away from the bones.

This dish makes a lot of pan gravy. Serve with hot cooked rice, hot mashed potatoes or hot cooked egg noodles to soak up the gravy. Any chicken pieces may be substituted for the chicken thighs.

Serves 30

"Just by being sent here by God and staying here has improved my situation. Praise God! This place is truly a God given blessing for me! My goals were met for saving money and staying sober."

Male Guest, Age 33

Crawfish Fettuccini

1 1/2 cups (3 sticks) butter
3 large onions, chopped
1 cup chopped celery
3 bell peppers, chopped
4 to 6 garlic cloves, crushed
1/4 cup all-purpose flour
2 cups half-and-half

16 ounces Velveeta cheese, chopped
1 tablespoon chopped jalapeño chile
Salt and pepper to taste
3 pounds crawfish tails
16 ounces fettuccini
2 cups (8 ounces) freshly grated
    Parmesan cheese

Melt the butter in a large heavy skillet over medium-high heat. Add the onions, celery, bell peppers and garlic and sauté for 15 minutes or until tender. Add the flour and cook for 2 minutes, stirring frequently. Reduce the heat to medium-low. Add the half-and-half gradually, stirring constantly. Cook for 10 minutes, stirring occasionally. Stir in the Velveeta cheese and jalapeño chile. Season with salt and pepper. Cook until the cheese is melted and combined, stirring occasionally. Stir in the crawfish tails and cook for 3 minutes. Remove from the heat.

Cook the pasta according to the package directions in a large saucepan. Drain the pasta and return to the saucepan. Stir in the crawfish mixture. Spoon into two 9×13-inch baking dishes sprayed with nonstick cooking spray. Sprinkle with the Parmesan cheese. Bake at 350 degrees for 20 minutes.

Serves 20

"I have found a job; now I am working on finding an apartment."

Female Guest, Age 25

Pulled Pork Barbecue Sandwiches

3 (7- to 8-pound) Boston butt pork roasts
2 (40-ounce) bottles hickory-smoked barbecue sauce
60 hamburger buns

Trim the pork of excess fat. Place on racks in large roasting pans. Bake, uncovered, at 500 degrees for 5 to 10 minutes. Decrease the temperature to 325 degrees. Bake for 5 to 6 hours or until the meat falls away from the bones. Let stand to cool enough to handle.

Remove and discard the bones. Pull and shred the pork with a large fork, discarding any excess fat and gristle. Place the shredded meat in the bottom of clean roasting pans. Pour one-half to three-fourths of the barbecue sauce over the meat. Toss until the pork is coated with the sauce. Bake at 350 degrees for 30 to 40 minutes. Serve on the hamburger buns as sandwiches. Serve the remaining sauce on the side.

The cooked and shredded pork may be frozen. Thaw completely before continuing as directed.

Serves 60

"The shelter helped me with saving money and legal advice. When I leave here my head will be on straight and I will be working and going to school to be an architect."

Female Guest, Age 21

Marinated Black Beans

^{1}/3 cup red wine vinegar
^{1}/3 cup olive oil
3 garlic cloves, crushed
^{3}/4 teaspoon salt
^{1}/2 teaspoon freshly ground pepper
3 (15-ounce) cans black beans, drained and rinsed
1 (10-ounce) package frozen corn kernels, thawed
1 large red onion, chopped
1 large red bell pepper, chopped
1 green bell pepper, chopped
Chopped fresh parsley (optional)

Whisk the vinegar, olive oil, garlic, salt and pepper together in a bowl. Let stand for 30 minutes. Combine the beans, corn, onion, red bell pepper and green bell pepper in a large bowl. Pour the vinaigrette over the bean mixture and toss to mix. Chill, covered, for 8 hours, tossing occasionally. Sprinkle with chopped fresh parsley and mix well. This recipe may be doubled.

Serves 10 to 15

"*The shelter helped me by getting my kids in school and providing them with supplies and uniforms. I'm taking more responsibility for my own actions.*"

Male Guest, Age 49

Boston Baked Beans

1 pound bacon, chopped
6 onions, chopped
6 large green bell peppers, chopped
6 (20-ounce) cans pork and beans

3 teaspoons chili powder
3/4 cup packed brown sugar
6 tablespoons molasses
1 1/2 cups ketchup

Cook the bacon in a skillet over medium-high heat until crisp. Remove with a slotted spoon to a dish, reserving the drippings in the skillet. Add the onions and bell peppers to the drippings and sauté until tender. Combine the bacon, onion mixture, pork and beans, chili powder, brown sugar, molasses and ketchup in a large bowl. Mix well and divide among two 9×13-inch baking dishes. Bake, covered, at 325 degrees for 1 hour. Bake, uncovered, for 1 hour longer or until thickened.

Serves 25

"*I have a safe place to stay for the night.*"

Female Guest, Age 26

Green Beans with Tasso

1 to 2 pounds tasso, chopped
32 cups water
1 large onion, chopped
2 to 4 teaspoons salt

4 teaspoons pepper
8 pounds frozen whole or cut
   green beans

Combine the tasso, water, onion, salt and pepper in a 12-quart stockpot. Bring to a boil and stir in the green beans. Return to a boil and simmer, uncovered, for 1 hour or until of the desired tenderness.

Serves 30

"*My homeless experience has been a learning experience.*"

Female Guest, Age 45

Red Beans and Rice

1¹/2 to 2 pounds ham bone with meat
4 cups frozen seasoning blend (onion, bell pepper and celery)
2 garlic cloves, chopped
2 pounds dried red beans
18 cups (or more) water
2 bay leaves
2 teaspoons liquid crab boil
Salt and pepper to taste
Hot cooked rice

Trim the meat and a small portion of fat from the ham bone. Cook the trimmed meat and fat in a skillet over medium-high heat until the fat is rendered down. Remove the meat with a slotted spoon to a plate, reserving the drippings in the pan. Add the vegetable blend and garlic to the drippings and sauté for 8 minutes or until tender.

Rinse and sort the beans. Combine the beans and water in a large stockpot and bring to a boil. Reduce the heat to low and add the ham meat, sautéed vegetables, bay leaves and crab boil. Cook, covered, for 1¹/2 to 2 hours or until the beans are tender, adding additional water if needed. Season with salt and pepper.

For a creamy consistency, remove 1 cup of the beans to a blender and process until smooth. Stir back into the remaining beans. Serve over the hot cooked rice.

The better the ham, the better the beans. Use the bone from a spiral-sliced honey-baked ham when available. It is sometimes possible to buy just the ham bone with the meat attached.

Serves 20

Red beans and rice is a popular Louisiana dish, traditionally served on Mondays using the ham bone left over from the previous Sunday's ham dinner. Many purists choose the small South Louisiana red beans over red kidney beans.

Hot German Potato Salad

10 pounds red potatoes
1 cup packed light brown sugar
2 cups cider vinegar
8 ounces bacon
14 ounces frozen seasoning blend, thawed
   (onion, bell pepper and celery)

Combine the potatoes and enough water to cover in a large saucepan or stockpot and bring to a boil. Boil until the potatoes are tender; drain. Let stand to cool just enough to handle. Slice the potatoes into thin rounds and place in a 4-quart bowl. Dissolve the brown sugar in the vinegar in a small saucepan over medium heat. Pour over the warm potatoes and toss to mix. This may be made ahead and chilled, covered tightly, until serving time.

Cook the bacon in a skillet over medium-high heat until crisp. Remove with a slotted spoon to a paper towel-lined plate to drain, reserving 3/4 cup drippings in the skillet. Crumble the bacon. Add the vegetable blend to the drippings and sauté until the onions begin to brown. Add the bacon and vegetable blend to the potatoes and mix well.

If the potato mixture has been chilled, place in a 4-quart baking dish and bake at 250 degrees until heated through. Continue as directed.

Serves 30

"The shelter helped me save money which I didn't have, paid out some bills and helped restore my transportation."

Male Guest, Age 48

184

Potato Salad

5 pounds red potatoes, peeled
6 to 8 eggs
$^1/_4$ cup sweet pickle relish
$^1/_4$ cup dill pickle relish
$^1/_4$ cup green olives, sliced
$^3/_4$ cup chopped celery
$1^1/_2$ cups (or more) mayonnaise
2 tablespoons yellow mustard
Salt and pepper to taste

Combine the potatoes and enough water to cover by 2 inches in a large saucepan or stockpot. Bring to a rolling boil. Boil until fork-tender; drain. Let stand for 10 minutes.

Combine the eggs and enough water to cover by 2 inches in a saucepan. Cover and bring to a boil. Remove from the heat and let stand for 15 minutes; drain. Place the eggs in a bowl of cold water; drain. Peel and chop the eggs.

Combine the potatoes, eggs, sweet pickle relish, dill pickle relish, olives, celery, mayonnaise and mustard in a bowl and mix well. Season with salt and pepper. Chill, covered, for 4 to 10 hours or until serving time. Add additional mayonnaise as needed to moisten the salad.

Serves 15 to 20

"I don't think the shelter and the personnel of the shelter could have done any better of a job than they have already done towards helping me."

Male Guest, Age 40

Coleslaw

1 (3-pound) package shredded
   cabbage with carrots
1 large red onion, thinly sliced
1 large red bell pepper, chopped
1 cup white vinegar

1 cup vegetable oil
1/2 cup sugar
1 teaspoon salt
1 teaspoon freshly ground pepper

Combine the cabbage, onion and bell pepper in a large bowl. Whisk the vinegar, oil, sugar, salt and pepper together in a small bowl. Pour over the cabbage mixture and toss to coat. Chill, covered, for 6 hours. Mix well before serving.

Serves 25 to 30

"I've learned patience and to think before acting and to care a little more about others' feelings."

Male Guest, Age 40

Garlic Cheese Bread

3 (1-pound) loaves Italian or
   French bread
1 1/2 cups (3 sticks) butter, softened
8 garlic cloves, minced

1/4 cup chopped fresh parsley
1 cup (4 ounces) freshly grated
   Parmesan cheese

Slice the bread into halves horizontally and arrange on foil-lined heavy duty baking sheets. Mix the butter, garlic and parsley in a bowl. Spread over the cut sides of the bread. Bake at 350 degrees for 10 minutes. Sprinkle with the cheese. Broil on high on the top rack for 2 to 3 minutes or until the edges of the bread begin to brown and the cheese is bubbly. Cool on the baking sheets for 1 minute. Slice each half into ten pieces.

Serves 30

"The shelter allowed me to save money to one day get my own place."

Male Guest, Age 48

Mexican Creamed Corn Bread

3 cups buttermilk
6 eggs, lightly beaten
3/4 cup canola oil
1 1/2 cups sour cream
3 cups canned cream-style corn
3 (4-ounce) cans chopped green chiles, drained
3/4 cup finely chopped onion
3 cups (12 ounces) shredded sharp Cheddar cheese
3 cups yellow cornmeal
1 1/2 cups all-purpose flour
3 tablespoons baking powder
1 1/2 teaspoons salt
3/4 teaspoon baking soda

Mix the buttermilk, eggs and canola oil in a large bowl until smooth. Stir in the sour cream, corn, green chiles and onion. Mix the cheese, cornmeal, flour, baking powder, salt and baking soda in a bowl. Add to the buttermilk mixture and stir just until combined. Divide between two 10×15-inch baking pans lined with greased baking parchment.

Bake at 350 degrees for 30 to 40 minutes or until slightly brown and firm to the touch. Cool in the pans for 10 minutes. Cut each pan into fifteen pieces.

Serves 20 to 30

"It's a nice place."

Female Guest on her first night in the Sweet Dreams Shelter, Age 6

Banana Pudding

4 (3-ounce) packages French vanilla instant pudding mix
7 cups milk
1 (14-ounce) can sweetened condensed milk
8 ounces cream cheese, softened
8 ounces whipped topping
5 bananas, sliced
1 (12-ounce) package vanilla wafers

Combine the pudding mix and milk in a bowl. Stir until the mixture is smooth and creamy. Let stand for 10 minutes. Mix the condensed milk, cream cheese and half the whipped topping in a bowl until smooth. Fold into the pudding. Fold in the bananas. Spoon a small amount of the banana mixture over the bottom of a 9×12-inch dish. Layer with one-half of the vanilla wafers, one-half of the remaining pudding mixture, the remaining vanilla wafers, the remaining pudding mixture and the remaining whipped topping. Chill, covered, until serving time.

Serves 20

"When I didn't have a family, Bishop Ott was my family."

Female Guest, mother of 3, Age 30

Blackberry Cobbler

4 pounds frozen blackberries, thawed
2 cups water
1/4 to 1/2 cup sugar
4 cups baking mix
1/2 cup sugar
1 cup (2 sticks) butter, melted

Arrange the blackberries in an 11×16-inch baking dish. Pour the water over the top and sprinkle with 1/4 to 1/2 cup sugar. Mix the baking mix and 1/2 cup sugar in a bowl. Add the butter and mix until crumbly. Sprinkle over the blackberries. Bake at 350 degrees for 1 hour. Serve warm with whipped cream or vanilla ice cream.

Serves 30

"Home base provides opportunities to improve ourselves."

Female Guest, Age 26

White Cake with Praline Frosting

Cake
1 (2-layer) package white cake mix
1 cup buttermilk
1/3 cup butter, melted
4 egg whites
1/4 teaspoon vanilla extract

Praline Frosting
2 cups packed brown sugar
2/3 cup whipping cream
1/2 cup (1 stick) butter
2 cups confectioners' sugar, sifted
2 teaspoons vanilla extract
13/4 cups chopped pecans, toasted

To prepare the cake, combine the cake mix, buttermilk, butter, egg whites and vanilla in a mixing bowl. Beat on low speed for 30 seconds. Scrape down the side of the bowl. Beat on low speed for 2 minutes longer. Pour into a baking parchment-lined 10×15-inch cake pan. Bake at 350 degrees for 15 to 20 minutes or until a wooden skewer inserted in the center comes out clean. Cool in the pan on a wire rack for 2 hours.

To prepare the frosting, combine the brown sugar, cream and butter in a saucepan. Bring to a boil, stirring often. Boil for 2 minutes. Remove from the heat and whisk in the confectioners' sugar and vanilla. Stir in the pecans. Stir gently for 5 to 8 minutes or until the frosting is slightly cool and begins to thicken. Pour over the cooled cake. Let cool completely and slice into fifteen pieces.

Serves 15

"This place will help you if you let it help you."

Female Guest, Age 36

Carrot Cake

Cake

1 (2-layer) package carrot cake mix
1/2 cup water
1/2 cup canola oil
4 eggs, lightly beaten
1 (8-ounce) can crushed pineapple
1/2 cup chopped walnuts or pecans
1/2 cup shredded coconut
1/2 cup dried cranberries or raisins

Frosting

8 ounces cream cheese, softened
1/2 cup (1 stick) butter, softened
1 (1-pound) package confectioners' sugar
1/2 cup chopped walnuts or pecans
1 teaspoon vanilla extract

To prepare the cake, combine the cake mix, water, canola oil, eggs and pineapple in a mixing bowl. Beat at low speed for 30 seconds. Scrape down the side of the bowl. Beat at medium speed for 2 minutes longer. Fold in the walnuts, coconut and cranberries. Pour into a baking parchment-lined 10 x15-inch cake pan. Bake at 350 degrees for 20 to 25 minutes or until a wooden skewer inserted in the center comes out clean. Let cool completely in the cake pan.

To prepare the frosting, beat the cream cheese and butter in a mixing bowl at medium speed until smooth. Add the confectioners' sugar and beat until light and creamy. Stir in the walnuts and vanilla. Spread over the top of the cooled cake. Cut into fifteen pieces.

Serves 15

"The shelter helped me in getting back on the right track with God."

Female Guest, Age 54

Appendix

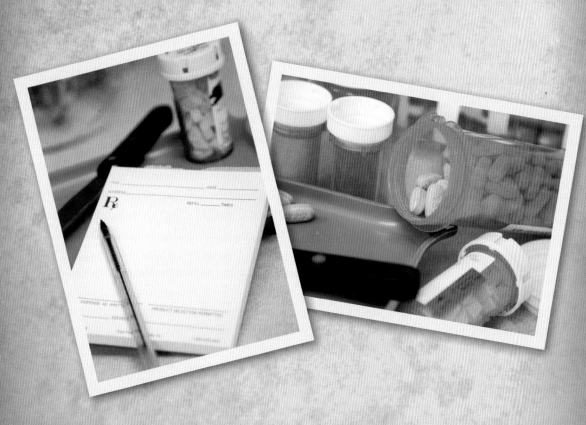

PRESCRIPTIONS OF LOVE

The St. Vincent de Paul Community Pharmacy provides life-sustaining medications for people who cannot afford them. Before seeking help at our pharmacy, some of our clients had been breaking tablets in half or even skipping doses of critical medications to make ends meet. The following story, which shows what one person learned about measuring love, is based on the experience of a Community Pharmacy staff member.

"As a member of the support staff at the community pharmacy, I often saw the pharmacists carefully measure out medicines. While I never considered love specifically in terms of a pharmacy commodity, I acted at times as if love was something to be measured and meted out carefully. That was before I met one particular couple at the pharmacy, who taught me a thing or two about the true measure of love.

"The first day this couple came to the pharmacy, the husband had just been released from the hospital, could barely walk, and had to lean heavily on his wife. As part of their initial visit, we learned that they had both been prescribed the same expensive but critically important heart medication. Since they couldn't afford to fill both prescriptions every month, their solution had been to take turns: the wife would take the medicine for one month, and the husband would take it the next. Their 'solution,' born of financial necessity, hadn't worked, and the husband's health had declined to the point that he had to be hospitalized.

"Once we started filling prescriptions for them, the husband's health improved, and before long, he was back to doing those things for his wife that he'd always enjoyed. He started opening doors for her again, and he seemed to take pleasure in getting her seated comfortably before signing in for both of them.

"From the first, it was obvious that this couple's love for each other had no defined edges, no fixed boundaries, and therefore defied measurement. From their kindness to each other in the smallest things to the depth of the sacrifices each was willing to make for the other, I saw that their love for one another wasn't measured and cautiously meted out; it was lavished, the way Jesus lavished his love on mankind. I'm just grateful to have had the opportunity to be part of their lives, a witness to unbounded love in action, and a small part of the answer to their prayers."

Pharmacy Staff Member

ABBREVIATIONS & EQUIVALENTS

Abbreviations

tsp.	teaspoon	oz.	ounce or ounces
pt.	pint	pkt.	packet(s)
T.	tablespoon	lb.	pound(s)
qt.	quart	mg	milligram(s)
c.	cup	btl.	bottle(s)
env.	envelope(s)	gm	gram(s)

Measurement Equivalents

a pinch	$1/8$ tsp. or less	8 ounces	1 cup
3 teaspoons	1 tablespoon	2 cups	1 pint
2 tablespoons	$1/8$ cup	2 pints	1 quart
4 tablespoons	$1/4$ cup	1 quart	4 cups
8 tablespoons	$1/2$ cup	4 quarts	1 gallon
1 jigger	$1^1/2$ ounces		

Equivalents

1 pound loaf bread	14 regular or 20 thin slices
28 saltines	1 cup fine crumbs
15 graham crackers	1 cup fine crumbs
22 vanilla wafers	1 cup fine crumbs
1 ounce butter	2 tablespoons
$1/2$ stick butter	$1/4$ cup
4 ounces cheese	1 cup shredded
1 pound cheese	4 cups shredded
1 ounce cream cheese	2 tablespoons
1 medium lemon	3 tablespoons juice
1 medium lemon	1 tablespoon grated zest
1 orange	$1/3$ cup juice
1 orange	2 tablespoons grated zest
1 pound raisins	$2^3/4$ cups

Give and gifts will be given to you; a good measure, packed together, shaken down, and overflowing, will be poured into your lap. For the measure with which you measure will in return be measured out to you.

Luke 6:38

HELPFUL KITCHEN HINTS

- Garbage disposer blades can be sharpened by running ice cubes through them.

- Place plastic wrap in refrigerator to prevent it from clinging to itself.

- Refrigerator and freezer odors can sometimes be eliminated by rubbing interior surfaces with a few drops of vanilla extract diluted in a cup of water.

- After thawing, check to see if meat or poultry still contains ice crystals. If it does, you can refreeze safely. Otherwise, the meat or poultry should be cooked.

- When sautéing meats, be careful not to overcrowd the pan. If there are too many pieces in the pan, the meat will steam instead of brown.

- When cooking red meat, turn the meat over to brown the other side when juices bubble to the surface of the meat.

- Basting the chicken during the last 30 minutes of cooking will allow the sauce to penetrate the chicken without browning the meat too quickly.

- By thawing frozen fish in milk it is possible to eliminate the frozen taste.

- To determine the ripeness of a watermelon, thump your index finger against it. A high "plink" means the melon is not ripe. A low "plunk" means it is ripe.

- Store strawberries in the refrigerator in a colander. This allows cold air to circulate in and around them keeping them fresher longer.

- To remove the silk from corn on the cob, rub with a damp paper towel.

- Pineapple juice can be used to preserve the color of sliced fresh fruits.

- To maintain the whiteness and the firmness of mushrooms while sautéing them, add a teaspoon of lemon juice for every quarter pound of melted butter.

- The quickest way to peel sweet potatoes is to boil them until just tender and then drop them into cold water. The skins will slip right off.

- For a cleaner cut when slicing brownies or cakes use a plastic knife.

- It is easier to grate any soft cheese if chilled in freezer before grating.

- To hasten the ripening of tomatoes or avocados, store them in a brown paper bag at room temperature.

- Chili powder, paprika, and red peppers deteriorate under humid and hot conditions. Store them in dark containers during the summer.

- Any dish that is prepared to serve cold should be slightly overseasoned because chilling subdues the seasonings.

- Store butter in the butter keeper or on the bottom shelf of the refrigerator. Otherwise, it will absorb flavors from other foods.

- Tomatoes will peel easily with a knife if you first let them stand in boiling water for 1 minute.

- Lettuce and celery will stay fresh longer if stored in a paper bag instead of plastic wrap.

- Lettuce will stay fresher longer if you store in the refrigerator without washing. Wash the day of use.

- Buy mushrooms with stems and caps attached rather than sliced and they will stay fresher longer.

- You'll get more juice from a lemon if first warmed in microwave for 20 seconds.

- To prevent rice or spaghetti from sticking, add a teaspoon of oil or butter to the boiling water while cooking.

- The shells of fresh eggs are rough and chalky; shells of old eggs are smooth and shiny.

- To determine whether an egg is hard-boiled, spin it. If it spins, it is hard-boiled; a raw egg will not spin.

- Eggshells can be easily removed from hard-boiled eggs if quickly rinsed under cold water first.

- The color of the eggshell has nothing to do with the taste or nutritional value.

- Use greased muffin cups as molds when baking stuffed green peppers.

- Before placing in the oven, add a cup of water to the bottom portion of the broiler pan to absorb smoke and grease.

- A bone-in roast will cook faster than a boneless roast. The bone carries the heat to the inside of the roast.

- After stewing a chicken, let it cool in the broth before removing the meat for more flavor.

- For moister hamburgers, add cold water to the meat before grilling (2 to 4 tablespoons per 1 pound of meat).

- To remove excess fat from soup or stew, add a few lettuce leaves. The fat will cling to the lettuce, which you can then discard.
- To allow steam to escape or to prevent grease from spattering, invert a metal colander over the frying pan.
- Dried herbs and spices may be substituted for fresh but they are more concentrated; use only one-third the amount.
- To make buttermilk, add 1 tablespoon lemon juice or vinegar to enough milk to make 1 cup. Let stand 5 minutes.
- It is easier to frost a cake that has been chilled first.
- When whipping cream, make sure the cream, bowl, and beaters are chilled. This will allow the cream to whip quicker.
- For a fluffier meringue, try adding ¼ teaspoon of cream of tartar.
- Reduce oven temperature by 25 degrees when using glass baking dishes.
- The finish on pans with nonstick coatings such as Teflon will be more durable if washed by hand rather than in the dishwasher.
- If the recipe calls for a 1-quart baking dish, a 9-inch pie plate or 8-inch cake pan may be substituted.
- If the recipe calls for a 2-quart baking dish, a 7×11-inch baking dish or a 5x9-inch loaf pan may be substituted.
- If the recipe calls for a 3-quart baking dish, a 9×13-inch baking pan may be substituted.

You are the salt of the earth. But if salt loses its taste, with what can it be seasoned? It is no longer good for anything but to be thrown out and trampled underfoot.

Matthew 5:13

Going Green in the Kitchen

Taking simple, inexpensive steps to reduce energy use will help your pocketbook and reduce your carbon footprint. Using fewer chemical-based cleansers is better for the environment and will save you money. Here are some helpful hints for "going green" in the kitchen.

- Be sure to place the faucet lever on the kitchen sink in the cold position when using small amounts of water; placing the lever in the hot position uses energy to heat the water even though it may never reach the faucet.

- Adding an aerator to your faucet reduces the amount of water you'll use in the kitchen for hand washing and dish rinsing.

- Don't leave the water running. Turn the faucet off when you're not using it.

- Keep range-top burners and reflectors clean; they will reflect the heat better, and you will save energy.

- Use a covered kettle or pan to boil water; it's faster and uses less energy.

- Match the size of the pan to the heating element.

- Whenever possible, use a microwave, toaster oven, pressure cooker or slow cooker instead of a standard electric oven. They won't use as much electricity and won't heat up your kitchen.

- Be sure your dishwasher is full when you run it, and don't bother to prerinse the dishes.

- Let dishes air dry, whether you wash them in the sink or the dishwasher.

- Did you know that refrigerators with the freezer on top are more efficient than those with freezers on the side?

- Don't keep your refrigerator too cold. Recommended temperatures are 37°F to 40°F for the fresh food compartment and 5°F for the freezer section.

- Cover liquids and wrap foods stored in the refrigerator. Uncovered foods release moisture and make the compressor work harder.

- Lower the thermostat on your hot water heater to 120°F.

- Use energy efficient fluorescent lights in fixtures.

- Combine shopping and errands into one trip.

- Shop your local farmers market.

- Plant a backyard garden. Growing herbs on your patio is a start.

- Compost fruits, vegetables, and coffee grounds. Keep a small, washable container (with a lid) in your kitchen for onion peels, carrot tops, apple cores, etc. At the end of the day, dump the contents into a bottomless bin in your backyard. Add leaves, grass clippings, and even shredded newspapers. Turn your compost once a week to aerate and soon it will look like dark rich soil that you can use in your garden.

- Bring your own bags to the supermarket. Buy several sturdy canvas or mesh bags that you can use over and over again.

- Reuse items such as grocery bags and glass jars.

- Bottled water is expensive in more ways than one. It hits your pocketbook pretty hard, but it also requires fuel to transport, and there are already too many plastic bottles in landfills. Use tap water instead. If you're concerned about water purity, buy a water filter. In the long run, you'll still save money.

- Purchase items in bulk to reduce the amount of packaging. This will also reduce the number of trips you have to make to the store.

- Double a recipe and freeze half for another meal.

- Baking soda is inexpensive and a great cleaner for cutting boards, kitchen counters, refrigerators and stove tops. In fact, baking soda and elbow grease will clean almost anything.

- Make a paste of baking soda and water to remove countertop stains like grape juice.

- An open box of baking soda in your refrigerator or freezer helps to remove odors.

- When you replace the box of baking soda in your refrigerator, pour it down your sink followed by a cup of vinegar. It will help to keep your pipes clean and fresh.

- Activated charcoal also helps to remove refrigerator odors. (You can find this in the pet supply section of the store.) Just spread about three ounces on a cookie sheet or shallow pan and place on a shelf in the refrigerator. (Note: It's okay for food to remain in the refrigerator with the charcoal.)

- To remove baked-on food from casserole dishes, add 3 tablespoons salt and 1 cup of boiling water. Let the dish stand until the water cools, then wash as usual.

- Use cloth dishtowels. Limit the use of paper towels.

- Remove stains from your coffee pot by putting 1 cup of water and 4 teaspoons of salt in the pot. Swirl the mixture around. Rinse and wash as usual.

INDEX

ALMONDS
Fruity Coleslaw, 67
Hot Chicken Salad, 89
Orange-Glazed Carrots, 111
Pan-Fried Red Snapper with
  Artichokes and Mushrooms, 76
Passover Cake, 147
Roasted Red Pepper Pesto, 45
Spinach and Strawberry Salad, 66

ANCHOVIES
Baguettes Rockefeller, 48
Tapenade, 46

ANDOUILLE
Cider-Glazed Pork Chops with
  Sweet Potato and Andouille Hash, 92
Louisiana Seafood Gumbo, 24
Pan-Seared Trout with Crab Meat
  Garlic Beurre Blanc, 19
Smoked Wood Duck and Andouille Gumbo, 25

APPETIZERS. *See also* Dips; Snacks; Spreads
Baguettes Rockefeller, 48
Crawfish Cheesecake, 37
Crawfish in a Bundle, 83
Kahlúa Grapes, 48
Layered Crab Dip, 38
Miniature Muffulettas, 40
Pepperoni Pinwheels, 41
Shrimp Nachos, 39
Zucchini Squares, 42

APPLE
Cider-Glazed Pork Chops with
  Sweet Potato and Andouille Hash, 92
4-4-4 Fruit Punch, 50
Fresh Apple Cake, 152
Pork Chops with Apple Cream Sauce, 93

ARTICHOKES
Mushroom Artichoke Soup, 60
Pan-Fried Red Snapper with
  Artichokes and Mushrooms, 76
Party Spinach, 127
Potato and Artichoke Casserole, 121
Sherried Artichoke Chicken, 89

AVOCADO
Guacamole, 39

BACON
Blue Cheese Dip, 44
Boston Baked Beans, 182
Cabbage Casserole, 110
Claire's Baked Duck Liver Pâté, 26
Curried Rice, 134
Hot German Potato Salad, 184
Mardi Gras Broccoli Salad, 64
Poor Man's Salad, 65
Sweet Potato Casserole, 125
Tailgate Party Beans, 109

BANANA
Banana Pudding, 188
Easy Fruit Salad, 67

BARBECUE
Barbecued Shrimp Longman, 21
Barbecue Sauce, 99
Beef Brisket with Barbecue Sauce, 99
Dry-Rubbed Baby Back Ribs, 96
Pulled Pork Barbecue Sandwiches, 180

BEANS. *See also* Black Beans; Green Beans
Bean Salad, 63
Boston Baked Beans, 182
Pasta e Fagioli Soup, 175
Red Beans and Rice, 183
Shrimp Nachos, 39
Speckled Butter Beans with Corn Bread
  Crust, 107
Taco Soup, 59
Tailgate Party Beans, 109
Vegetable Casserole, 131

BEEF. *See also* Ground Beef
Bayouland Beef Stew with Vegetables, 31
Beef Brisket with Barbecue Sauce, 99
Corned Beef and Vegetables, 100
French Dip Sandwiches, 101
Grecian Skillet Rib-Eye Steaks, 98
Grillades, 102

BEVERAGES. *See also* Champagne
Bayou Blue Tea, 51
Café au Lait with a Punch, 52
Double Irish Coffee, 52
4-4-4 Fruit Punch, 50
Peach Spritzers, 49
Spicy Bloody Mary Mix, 49

Wedding Punch, 50
White Chocolate Latte, 51

BLACK BEANS
Black Bean and Feta Dip, 45
Marinated Black Beans, 181
Southwestern Corn and Black Bean Salad, 63

BLACKBERRY
Blackberry Cobbler, 188
Meringue Shells with Fresh Berries, 150

BLUEBERRY
Bayou Blue Tea, 51
Meringue Shells with Fresh Berries, 150

BREAD PUDDINGS
Piña Colada Bread Pudding, 144
Spinach and Monterey Jack Bread Pudding, 126
Sweet Potato Bread Pudding, 143

BREADS. *See also* Corn Bread
Asphodel Bread, 69
Baguettes Rockefeller, 48
Basil Biscuits, 85
Beignets, 141
Garlic Cheese Bread, 186
Italian Olive Bread, 69
King Cake, 154
Pumpkin Bread, 70
Sfinges, 142
Shortcake Biscuits, 34
Upside-Down French Toast, 70

BROCCOLI
Broccoli with Caper Sauce, 110
Mardi Gras Broccoli Salad, 64
Shelter Scramble Squares, 41

BUTTERS
Pecan Butter, 75
Shrimp Butter, 38

CABBAGE
Cabbage Casserole, 110
Coleslaw, 186
Corned Beef and Vegetables, 100
Fruity Coleslaw, 67
Pasta e Fagioli Soup, 175
Southwestern Corn and Black Bean
    Salad, 63

CAJUN, 25, 55, 84, 85
Boudin Blanc, 33

Cuisine, 31
Louisiana Seafood Gumbo, 24

CAKES
Baba, 148
Carrot Cake, 190
Coca-Cola Cake, 153
Cranberry Upside-Down Cake, 156
Fresh Apple Cake, 152
King Cake, 154
Passover Cake, 147
Pecan Date Fruitcake, 157
White Cake with Praline Frosting, 189

CANDY
Chocolate Toffee Bars, 167
Creamy Pralines, 166
Divinity Fudge, 165
Peanut Brittle, 167
Peanut Butter Fudge, 165
Pralines, 166

CANE SYRUP
Pork Medallions Louisianne, 95
Sweet Potato Bread Pudding, 143
Traditional Venison Jerky, 30

CAPERS
Broccoli with Caper Sauce, 110
Caponatina, 47
Tapenade, 46

CARROTS
Bayouland Beef Stew with
    Vegetables, 31
Carrot Cake, 190
Corned Beef and Vegetables, 100
Marinated Carrot Salad, 64
Orange-Glazed Carrots, 111

CAULIFLOWER
Cauliflower Gratin, 112
Microwave Cauliflower, 111

CHAMPAGNE
Peach Spritzers, 49
Wedding Punch, 50

CHEESECAKES
Crawfish Cheesecake, 37
Pecan Cheesecake Pie, 159

CHERRY
Pecan Date Fruitcake, 157

CHICKEN
African Chicken, 87
Chicken and Pork Jambalaya, 176
Chicken Mole, 88
Chicken Salad, 62
Chicken Supreme, 90
Hot Chicken Salad, 89
Mama's Chicken Fricassee, 27
Mexican Chicken Stew, 177
Mushroom Chicken for a Crowd, 178
Rainy Day Chicken Soup, 58
Sherried Artichoke Chicken, 89

CHILES. *See also* Jalapeño Chiles
Chicken Mole, 88
Dirty Rice, 135
Mexican Creamed Corn Bread, 187
Potatoes Supreme, 121
Speckled Butter Beans with Corn Bread Crust, 107

CHOCOLATE. *See also* White Chocolate
Chicken Mole, 88
Chocolate Chess Pie, 159
Chocolate Chip Cheese Ball, 44
Chocolate Chunk Butter Pecan Ice Cream, 151
Chocolate Mousse Trifle, 145
Chocolate Toffee Bars, 167
Coca-Cola Cake, 153
Coca-Cola Chocolate Frosting, 153
Coconut Mounds, 171
Double Irish Coffee, 52
Holiday Oatmeal Cookies, 170
Passover Cake, 147
Peppermint Biscotti, 172
Strawberry Chocolate Cream Pie, 160
Strawberry Tiramisu, 149

CILANTRO
Black-Eyed Peas with Mushrooms, 117
Cider-Glazed Pork Chops with
    Sweet Potato and Andouille Hash, 92
Homemade Salsa, 39
Roasted Catfish with Sweet Potatoes and
    Corn Salad, 74
Roasted Red Pepper Pesto, 45
Shrimp Nachos, 39
Southwestern Corn and Black Bean Salad, 63

CLAMS
Louisiana Clam Chowder, 22

COCONUT
Baba, 148
Carrot Cake, 190

Coconut Mounds, 171
No-Bake Cake, 149
Pina Colada Bread Pudding, 144
Sweet Potato Casserole, 125

COOKIES
Coconut Mounds, 171
Holiday Oatmeal Cookies, 170
Macadamia Nut and White Chocolate Cookies, 168
Peppermint Biscotti, 172
Shade Tree Oatmeal Cookies, 169

CORN
Black Bean and Feta Dip, 45
Crawfish Corn Bread, 68
Father Jeff's Corn and Crab Meat Bisque, 55
Jalapeño Corn Bread, 68
Maque Choux, 113
Marinated Black Beans, 181
Mexican Creamed Corn Bread, 187
Roasted Catfish with Sweet Potatoes and
    Corn Salad, 74
Shelter Scramble Squares, 41
Southwestern Corn and Black Bean Salad, 63
Spicy Potato and Corn Casserole, 120
Taco Soup, 59

CORN BREAD
Crawfish Corn Bread, 68
Jalapeño Corn Bread, 68
Mexican Creamed Corn Bread, 187
Speckled Butter Beans with Corn Bread Crust, 107

COUSCOUS
Mushroom Couscous, 133

CRAB MEAT
Crab Cakes Rex, 20
Crab Meat and Shrimp over Cheese Grits, 78
Crab Meat Imperial, 77
Father Jeff's Corn and Crab Meat Bisque, 55
Layered Crab Dip, 38
Louisiana Seafood Gumbo, 24
Pan-Seared Trout with Crab Meat
    Garlic Beurre Blanc, 19

CRANBERRY
Carrot Cake, 190
Cranberry Upside-Down Cake, 156
Frozen Cranberry Salad, 66
Fruity Coleslaw, 67
Holiday Oatmeal Cookies, 170
Stuffed Sweet Potatoes, 124
Wild Rice Pilaf, 137

CRAWFISH
Atchafalaya Basin, Louisiana, 56
Blend of the Bayou, 81
Breaux Bridge, Louisiana, 82
Crawfish Boil Chowder, 56
Crawfish Cheesecake, 37
Crawfish Corn Bread, 68
Crawfish Étouffée with Basil Biscuits, 85
Crawfish Fettuccini, 179
Crawfish in a Bundle, 83
Crawfish Jambalaya, 84
Crawfish Pasta Salad, 61
Crawfish Pie, 82
Crawfish Remoulade Salad, 62
Crawfish Rice, 136
Louisiana-Style Crawfish Étouffée, 23

CREOLE, 166
Creole Cream Cheese Strawberry Shortcakes, 34
Creole Pork Chops, 94
Fried Turkey, 91
Louisiana-Style Crawfish Étouffée, 23
Maque Choux, 113
White Roux, 29

CURRY
Curried Okra, 115
Curried Rice, 134
Sweet Potato Fries with Mango Chutney
    Mayonnaise, 123

DESSERTS. *See also* Bread Puddings; Cakes; Candy;
    Cheesecakes; Cookies; Frostings/Glazes;
    Pies, Dessert
Banana Pudding, 188
Beignets, 141
Blackberry Cobbler, 188
Chocolate Chunk Butter Pecan Ice Cream, 151
Chocolate Mousse Trifle, 145
Creole Cream Cheese Strawberry
    Shortcakes, 34
Kahlúa Grapes, 48
Meringue Shells with Fresh Berries, 150
No-Bake Cake, 149
Sfinges, 142
Spanish Flan Dessert, 146
Strawberry Flambé, 150
Strawberry Tiramisu, 149

DIPS. *See also* Salsas
Black Bean and Feta Dip, 45
Blue Cheese Dip, 44
Guacamole, 39
Homemade Salsa, 39

Layered Crab Dip, 38
Olive Dip, 46

DRY RUBS
Beef Brisket with Barbecue Sauce, 99
Dry-Rubbed Baby Back Ribs, 96
Grecian Skillet Rib-Eye Steaks, 98

DUCK
Claire's Baked Duck Liver Pâté, 26
Smoked Wood Duck and Andouille
    Gumbo, 25

EGGPLANT
Caponatina, 47
Italian Vegetables, 130
Tahini Roasted Vegetables, 132

ETOUFFÉE
Crawfish Étouffée with Basil Biscuits, 85
Louisiana-Style Crawfish Étouffée, 23

FISH. *See also* Anchovies
Bass with Summer Squash, 73
Pan-Fried Red Snapper with
    Artichokes and Mushrooms, 76
Pan-Seared Trout with Crab Meat
    Garlic Beurre Blanc, 19
Roasted Catfish with Sweet Potatoes and
    Corn Salad, 74
Salmon Steaks with Pecan Butter, 75

FRENCH
Beignet, 141
Boudin, 33
Café au Lait, 52
Etouffée, 23, 85
French Dip Sandwiches, 101
King Cake, 155
Lagniappe, 37, 158
Maque Choux, 113
Upside-Down French Toast, 70

FROSTINGS/GLAZES, 154, 156, 190
Coca-Cola Chocolate Frosting, 153
Praline Frosting, 189
Vanilla Cream Cheese Frosting, 152

FRUIT. *See also* individual kinds; Salads, Fruit
Sweet Potato Fries with Mango Chutney
    Mayonnaise, 123

GAME. *See also* Duck; Venison
Quail with Mushroom Gravy, 90

GREEN BEANS
Bean Salad, 63
Chicken Supreme, 90
Curried Rice, 134
Green Beans with Tasso, 182
Not Your Mama's Green Bean Casserole, 108
Pasta e Fagioli Soup, 175
Vegetable Casserole, 131

GRILLED
Cider-Glazed Pork Chops with
    Sweet Potato and Andouille Hash, 92
Dry-Rubbed Baby Back Ribs, 96
Grilled Sweet Potatoes, 124
Salmon Steaks with Pecan Butter, 75

Grits, 78, 102

GROUND BEEF
Baked Spaghetti, 104
Dirty Rice, 135
Hamburger Soup, 59
Italian Sauce with Meatballs, 103
Natchitoches Meat Pies, 32
Pasta e Fagioli Soup, 175
Taco Soup, 59
Tailgate Party Beans, 109

GUMBO
Cultural, 87
Louisiana Seafood Gumbo, 24
Okra, 116
Smoked Wood Duck and Andouille Gumbo, 25

HAM
Miniature Muffulettas, 40
Red Beans and Rice, 183

JALAPEÑO CHILES
Crawfish Corn Bread, 68
Crawfish Fettuccini, 179
Guacamole, 39
Jalapeño Corn Bread, 68
Mexican Chicken Stew, 177
Roasted Catfish with Sweet Potatoes and
    Corn Salad, 74
Shrimp Nachos, 39

JAMBALAYA
Chicken and Pork Jambalaya, 176
Crawfish Jambalaya, 84

LAGNIAPPE, 37
Louisiana Lagniappe's Pecan Pie, 158

LIVER
Boudin Blanc, 33
Claire's Baked Duck Liver Pâté, 26

LOUISIANA
Atchafalaya Basin, Louisiana, 56
Breaux Bridge, Louisiana, 82
Louisiana Clam Chowder, 22
Louisiana Lagniappe's Pecan Pie, 158
Louisiana Seafood Gumbo, 24
Louisiana-Style Crawfish Étouffée, 23
LSU Human Ecology Department, 115
Mardi Gras, 64
Natchitoches Meat Pies, 32
Pelican State, The, 151
Red Beans and Rice, 183
Sportsman's Paradise, 90
Tony's Seafood, Donaldsville, Louisiana, 79

MIREPOIX, 55
Father Jeff's Corn and Crab Meat Bisque, 55
Hamburger Soup, 59
Mama's Chicken Fricassee, 27
Rainy Day Chicken Soup, 58

MUFFULETTAS
Miniature Muffulettas, 40
Muffuletta, 40

MUSHROOMS
African Chicken, 87
Baked Orzo with Fontina Cheese and Peas, 138
Bayouland Beef Stew with Vegetables, 31
Black-Eyed Peas with Mushrooms, 117
Blend of the Bayou, 81
Crawfish Jambalaya, 84
Crawfish Rice, 136
Creole Pork Chops, 94
Curried Rice, 134
Italian Vegetables, 130
Mama's Chicken Fricassee, 27
Mushroom Artichoke Soup, 60
Mushroom Chicken for a Crowd, 178
Mushroom Couscous, 133
Not Your Mama's Green Bean Casserole, 108
Pan-Fried Red Snapper with Artichokes and
    Mushrooms, 76
Pan-Seared Trout with Crab Meat Garlic
    Beurre Blanc, 19
Party Spinach, 127
Quail with Mushroom Gravy, 90
Rainy Day Chicken Soup, 58
Sautéed Mushrooms with Parsley, 114
Sherried Artichoke Chicken, 89

Shrimp Baton Rouge, 80
Spinach and Monterey Jack Bread Pudding, 126

NUTS. *See also* Almonds; Peanuts/Peanut Butter;
    Pecans; Pine Nuts; Walnuts
    Macadamia Nut and White Chocolate
      Cookies, 168

OKRA
    Curried Okra, 115
    Louisiana Seafood Gumbo, 24
    Smothered Okra and Tomatoes, 116

OLIVE
    Caponatina, 47
    Crawfish in a Bundle, 83
    Grecian Skillet Rib-Eye Steaks, 98
    Italian Olive Bread, 69
    Miniature Muffulettas, 40
    Olive Dip, 46
    Olive Pasta Salad, 65
    Pepperoni Pinwheels, 41
    Potato Salad, 185
    Tapenade, 46

ORANGE
    Easy Fruit Salad, 67
    4-4-4 Fruit Punch, 50
    Glaze, 156
    Medallions of Venison with Kumquat Glaze, 28
    Orange-Glazed Carrots, 111

OYSTERS
    Louisiana Seafood Gumbo, 24
    Oysters à la Mosca, 86

PASTA
    Baked Orzo with Fontina Cheese and
      Peas, 138
    Baked Spaghetti, 104
    Crawfish Fettuccini, 179
    Crawfish Pasta Salad, 61
    Crawfish Rice, 136
    Garlic White Lasagna, 97
    Hamburger Soup, 59
    Italian Sauce, 103
    Italian Sausage and Pepper Pasta, 96
    Mama's Chicken Fricassee, 27
    Olive Pasta Salad, 65
    Pasta e Fagioli Soup, 175
    Rainy Day Chicken Soup, 58
    Shrimp Baton Rouge, 80

Pastry, 32, 148, 164

PEACH
    Easy Fruit Salad, 67
    Peach Spritzers, 49

PEANUTS/PEANUT BUTTER
    African Chicken, 87
    Helenihi Pork Loin, 95
    Peanut Brittle, 167
    Peanut Butter Fudge, 165
    Sweet Potato Casserole, 125

PEAS
    Baked Orzo with Fontina Cheese and
      Peas, 138
    Black-Eyed Peas with Mushrooms, 117
    Crawfish Pasta Salad, 61
    Crawfish Rice, 136
    Olive Pasta Salad, 65
    Snap Peas with Roasted Garlic Dressing, 118
    Vegetable Casserole, 131

PECANS
    Carrot Cake, 190
    Chocolate Chip Cheese Ball, 44
    Chocolate Chunk Butter Pecan Ice Cream, 151
    Chocolate Mousse Trifle, 145
    Chocolate Toffee Bars, 167
    Crawfish Rice, 136
    Cream Cheese Frosting, 190
    Creamy Pralines, 166
    Divinity Fudge, 165
    Fresh Apple Cake, 152
    Frozen Cranberry Salad, 66
    Fruity Coleslaw, 67
    Holiday Oatmeal Cookies, 170
    Louisiana Lagniappe's Pecan Pie, 158
    Mardi Gras Broccoli Salad, 64
    Meringue Shells with Fresh Berries, 150
    Olive Dip, 46
    Pecan Butter, 75
    Pecan Cheesecake Pie, 159
    Pecan Date Fruitcake, 157
    Pork Medallions Louisianne, 95
    Praline Frosting, 189
    Praline Pumpkin Pie, 162
    Pralines, 166
    Praline Sauce, 143
    Shade Tree Oatmeal Cookies, 169
    Spinach and Strawberry Salad, 66
    Stuffed Sweet Potatoes, 124
    Sweet Potato Casserole, 125
    Upside-Down French Toast, 70
    Vanilla Cream Cheese Frosting, 152
    Wild Rice Pilaf, 137

PESTO
Roasted Red Pepper Pesto, 45
Sun-Dried Tomato and Pesto Torta, 43

PIES, DESSERT
Buttermilk Pie, 163
Chocolate Chess Pie, 159
Louisiana Lagniappe's Pecan Pie, 158
Never-Fail Pie Crust, 164
Pecan Cheesecake Pie, 159
Praline Pumpkin Pie, 162
Strawberry Chocolate Cream Pie, 160
Strawberry Pie, 161

PIES, SAVORY
Crawfish Pie, 82
Natchitoches Meat Pies, 32
Speckled Butter Beans with Corn Bread Crust, 107

PINEAPPLE
Carrot Cake, 190
Easy Fruit Salad, 67
4-4-4 Fruit Punch, 50
Frozen Cranberry Salad, 66
Fruity Coleslaw, 67
Helenihi Pork Loin, 95
No-Bake Cake, 149
Piña Colada Bread Pudding, 144
Scalloped Pineapple, 132
Sweet Potato Casserole, 125
Wedding Punch, 50

PINE NUTS
Southwestern Corn and Black Bean Salad, 63
Sun-Dried Tomato and Pesto Torta, 43

PORK. *See also* Bacon; Ham; Sausage
Boudin Blanc, 33
Chicken and Pork Jambalaya, 176
Cider-Glazed Pork Chops with
    Sweet Potato and Andouille Hash, 92
Creole Pork Chops, 94
Dry-Rubbed Baby Back Ribs, 96
Helenihi Pork Loin, 95
Natchitoches Meat Pies, 32
Pork Chops with Apple Cream Sauce, 93
Pork Medallions Louisianne, 95
Pulled Pork Barbecue Sandwiches, 180

POTATOES
Bayouland Beef Stew with Vegetables, 31
Corned Beef and Vegetables, 100
Garlic Mashed Potatoes, 119
Hot German Potato Salad, 184

Louisiana Clam Chowder, 22
Parmesan Scalloped Potatoes, 122
Potato and Artichoke Casserole, 121
Potatoes Supreme, 121
Potato Salad, 185
Rosemary and Goat Cheese Smashed Potatoes, 119
Spicy Potato and Corn Casserole, 120

PRALINE
Creamy Pralines, 166
Praline Frosting, 189
Praline Pumpkin Pie, 162
Pralines, 166
Praline Sauce, 143

PUMPKIN
Praline Pumpkin Pie, 162
Pumpkin Bread, 70

RAISIN
Carrot Cake, 190
Fruity Coleslaw, 67
Mardi Gras Broccoli Salad, 64
Shade Tree Oatmeal Cookies, 169

RASPBERRY
Raspberry Sauce, 147

RESTAURANTS
Asphodel Plantation, East Feliciana Parish, 69
Central Grocery, French Quarter, 40
Chef John Folse and Company, 22
Commander's Palace, New Orleans, 57
Louisiana Lagniappe, Baton Rouge, 158
Manale's Restaurant, New Orleans, 21
Mosca's, New Orleans, 86
Tony's Seafood, Donaldsville, Louisiana, 79

RICE
African Chicken, 87
Bayouland Beef Stew with Vegetables, 31
Blend of the Bayou, 81
Boudin Blanc, 33
Chicken and Pork Jambalaya, 176
Chicken Mole, 88
Chicken Supreme, 90
Crawfish Jambalaya, 84
Crawfish Rice, 136
Creole Pork Chops, 94
Curried Rice, 134
Dirty Rice, 135
Louisiana Seafood Gumbo, 24
Louisiana-Style Crawfish Étouffée, 23
Mama's Chicken Fricassee, 27

Mexican Chicken Stew, 177
Quail with Mushroom Gravy, 90
Red Beans and Rice, 183
Smoked Wood Duck and Andouille Gumbo, 25
Wild Rice Pilaf, 137

ROSEMARY
Rosemary and Goat Cheese Smashed
    Potatoes, 119

ROUX
Blond Roux, 29
Brown Roux, 29
Butter Roux, 29
White Roux, 29

SALAD DRESSINGS, 61

SALADS, FRUIT
Easy Fruit Salad, 67
Frozen Cranberry Salad, 66
Spinach and Strawberry Salad, 66

SALADS, MAIN DISH
Chicken Salad, 62
Crawfish Pasta Salad, 61
Crawfish Remoulade Salad, 62
Hot Chicken Salad, 89

SALADS, VEGETABLE
Bean Salad, 63
Coleslaw, 186
Fruity Coleslaw, 67
Hot German Potato Salad, 184
Mardi Gras Broccoli Salad, 64
Marinated Black Beans, 181
Marinated Carrot Salad, 64
Olive Pasta Salad, 65
Poor Man's Salad, 65
Potato Salad, 185
Roasted Catfish with Sweet Potatoes and
    Corn Salad, 74
Southwestern Corn and Black Bean Salad, 63

SALAMI
Miniature Muffulettas, 40

SALSAS
Homemade Salsa, 39

SANDWICHES. *See also* Muffulettas
Crawfish in a Bundle, 83
French Dip Sandwiches, 101
Pulled Pork Barbecue Sandwiches, 180

Roasted Red Pepper Pesto, 45
Shrimp Po' Boys, 79
Tomato Basil Bisque, 60

SAUCES. *See also* Pesto
Barbecue Sauce, 99
Beurre Blanc, 19
Broccoli with Caper Sauce, 110
Compound Butter, 19
Demi-Glace, 28
Horseradish Sauce, 100
Italian Sauce, 103
Pork Chops with Apple Cream Sauce, 93
Praline Sauce, 143
Raspberry Sauce, 147
Rum Sauce, 144

SAUSAGE. *See also* Andouille; Salami
Boudin Blanc, 33
Chicken and Pork Jambalaya, 176
Dirty Rice, 135
Garlic White Lasagna, 97
Green Beans with Tasso, 182
Italian Sausage and Pepper Pasta, 96
Miniature Muffulettas, 40
Pepperoni Pinwheels, 41

SEAFOOD. *See* Clams; Crab Meat; Crawfish; Fish;
    Oysters; Shellfish; Shrimp

SHRIMP
Barbecued Shrimp Longman, 21
Crab Meat and Shrimp over
    Cheese Grits, 78
Louisiana Seafood Gumbo, 24
Mirlitons with Shrimp, 129
Shrimp Baton Rouge, 80
Shrimp Butter, 38
Shrimp Nachos, 39
Shrimp Po' Boys, 79

SIDE DISHES
Cheese Grits, 78
Crawfish Rice, 136
Dirty Rice, 135
Mushroom Couscous, 133
Scalloped Pineapple, 132
Tabbouli, 134

SNACKS
Baguettes Rockefeller, 48
Kahlúa Grapes, 48
Miniature Muffulettas, 40
Pepperoni Pinwheels, 41

Shelter Scramble Squares, 41
Shrimp Nachos, 39
Traditional Venison Jerky, 30
Zucchini Squares, 42

SOUPS/STEWS. *See also* Étouffée; Gumbo; Jambalaya
Bayouland Beef Stew with Vegetables, 31
Commander's Palace Turtle Soup au Sherry, 57
Crawfish Boil Chowder, 56
Father Jeff's Corn and Crab Meat Bisque, 55
Hamburger Soup, 59
Louisiana Clam Chowder, 22
Mexican Chicken Stew, 177
Mushroom Artichoke Soup, 60
Pasta e Fagioli Soup, 175
Rainy Day Chicken Soup, 58
Taco Soup, 59
Tomato Basil Bisque, 60

SPINACH
Baguettes Rockefeller, 48
Garlic White Lasagna, 97
Party Spinach, 127
Spinach and Monterey Jack Bread Pudding, 126
Spinach and Strawberry Salad, 66

SPREADS. *See also* Butters
Caponatina, 47
Chocolate Chip Cheese Ball, 44
Claire's Baked Duck Liver Pâté, 26
Crawfish Cheesecake, 37
Roasted Red Pepper Pesto, 45
Shrimp Butter, 38
Sun-Dried Tomato and Pesto Torta, 43
Tapenade, 46

SQUASH
Bass with Summer Squash, 73
Italian Vegetables, 130
Mirlitons with Shrimp, 129
Squash Casserole, 128
Tahini Roasted Vegetables, 132

STRAWBERRY
Creole Cream Cheese Strawberry
   Shortcakes, 34
Easy Fruit Salad, 67
Meringue Shells with Fresh Berries, 150
Ponchatoula, 161
Spinach and Strawberry Salad, 66
Strawberry Chocolate Cream Pie, 160
Strawberry Flambé, 150
Strawberry Pie, 161
Strawberry Tiramisu, 149

SWEET POTATOES
Cider-Glazed Pork Chops with
   Sweet Potato and Andouille Hash, 92
Grilled Sweet Potatoes, 124
Roasted Catfish with Sweet Potatoes and
   Corn Salad, 74
Stuffed Sweet Potatoes, 124
Sweet Potato Bread Pudding, 143
Sweet Potato Casserole, 125
Sweet Potato Fries with Mango Chutney
   Mayonnaise, 123

TOMATOES
African Chicken, 87
Baked Spaghetti, 104
Black-Eyed Peas with Mushrooms, 117
Chicken and Pork Jambalaya, 176
Chicken Mole, 88
Commander's Palace Turtle Soup au Sherry, 57
Crawfish Étouffée with Basil Biscuits, 85
Crawfish Jambalaya, 84
Crawfish Pasta Salad, 61
Crawfish Rice, 136
Creole Pork Chops, 94
Grillades, 102
Guacamole, 39
Hamburger Soup, 59
Homemade Salsa, 39
Italian Sauce, 103
Italian Sausage and Pepper Pasta, 96
Italian Vegetables, 130
Layered Crab Dip, 38
Louisiana-Style Crawfish Étouffée, 23
Maque Choux, 113
Marinated Carrot Salad, 64
Mexican Chicken Stew, 177
Pasta e Fagioli Soup, 175
Poor Man's Salad, 65
Smothered Okra and Tomatoes, 116
Southwestern Corn and Black Bean Salad, 63
Spicy Bloody Mary Mix, 49
Spicy Potato and Corn Casserole, 120
Tabbouli, 134
Taco Soup, 59
Tomato Basil Bisque, 60

TOMATOES, SUN-DRIED
Mushroom Artichoke Soup, 60
Sun-Dried Tomato and Pesto Torta, 43

TRINITY, THE, 55
Chicken and Pork Jambalaya, 176
Crab Cakes Rex, 20
Crab Meat and Shrimp over Cheese Grits, 78

Crawfish Étouffée with Basil Biscuits, 85
Crawfish Fettuccini, 179
Crawfish Pie, 82
Creole Pork Chops, 94
Father Jeff's Corn and Crab Meat Bisque, 55
Grillades, 102
Louisiana Seafood Gumbo, 24
Louisiana-Style Crawfish Étouffée, 23
Mama's Chicken Fricassee, 27
Maque Choux, 113
Smoked Wood Duck and Andouille Gumbo, 25

Turkey, Fried, 91

Turtle Soup au Sherry, Commander's Palace, 57

VEGETABLES. *See also* individual kinds;
   Salads, Vegetable
Italian Vegetables, 130
Not Your Mama's Green Bean Casserole, 108
Tahini Roasted Vegetables, 132
Vegetable Casserole, 131

VENISON
Medallions of Venison with Kumquat Glaze, 28
Traditional Venison Jerky, 30

WALNUTS
Carrot Cake, 190
Cranberry Upside-Down Cake, 156
Cream Cheese Frosting, 190
Frozen Cranberry Salad, 66
Shelter Scramble Squares, 41

WHITE CHOCOLATE
Macadamia Nut and White Chocolate
   Cookies, 168
White Chocolate Latte, 51

ZUCCHINI
Bass with Summer Squash, 73
Italian Vegetables, 130
Tahini Roasted Vegetables, 132
Zucchini Squares, 42

TASTE ⚜ SEE is a perfect gift for holidays, weddings, anniversaries, and birthdays.
To order additional copies as gifts for your friends and family, please contact us at

Society of St. Vincent de Paul
P.O. Box 127
Baton Rouge, Louisiana 70821-0127

Phone: 225-383-7837
Fax: 225-383-6623
E-mail: cookbook@svdpbr.com
Web site: www.svdpbr.org